Messages from Her

Rachael McKee

Illustrations by Harley & J

Andrews McMeel
PUBLISHING®

Messages from Her copyright © 2023 by Rachael McKee. All rights reserved. Printed in China. No part of this book may be used or reproduced in any manner whatsoever without written permission except in the case of reprints in the context of reviews.

Andrews McMeel Publishing
a division of Andrews McMeel Universal
1130 Walnut Street, Kansas City, Missouri 64106

www.andrewsmcmeel.com

23 24 25 26 27 RLP 10 9 8 7 6 5 4 3 2 1

ISBN: 978-1-5248-8648-6

Editor: Cindy Harris
Art Director: Julie Barnes
Production Editor: Elizabeth A. Garcia
Production Manager: Tamara Haus

ATTENTION: SCHOOLS AND BUSINESSES
Andrews McMeel books are available at quantity discounts with bulk purchase for educational, business, or sales promotional use. For information, please e-mail the Andrews McMeel Publishing Special Sales Department: sales@amuniversal.com.

To all the women who came before me, thank you! I stand on your shoulders.

Contents

INTRODUCTION	6
WHY THESE 44 WOMEN?	7
WHO IS THIS BOOK & DECK FOR?	8
HOW TO USE THIS BOOK & DECK	9
CARD SPREADS	12

THE WOMEN
Amelia Earhart	16
Anne Frank	18
Annie Easley	20
Aretha Franklin	22
Beyoncé	24
Cher	26
Cyndi Lauper	28
Diana, Princess of Wales	30
Dolly Parton	32
Eleanor Roosevelt	34
Erykah Badu	36
Estée Lauder	38
Frida Kahlo	40
Georgia O'Keeffe	42
Gloria Gaynor	44
Gloria Steinem	46
Helen Keller	48

Irena Sendler	50
Jane Addams	52
Jane Goodall	54
Janelle Monáe	56
Julia Child	58
Julia Louis-Dreyfus	60
Lizzo	62
Madonna	64
Malala	66
Marie Curie	68
Marie Forleo	70
Marilyn Monroe	72
Martha Stewart	74
Maya Angelou	76
Michelle Obama	78
Nina Simone	80
Oprah Winfrey	82
Patsy Mink	84
Queen Elizabeth II	86
Rachel Carson	88
Ruth Bader Ginsburg	90
Sandra Day O'Connor	92
Serena & Venus Williams	94
Sylvia Rivera	96
Toni Morrison	98
Wilma Mankiller	100
You	102

Introduction

This is an introduction for women who need no introduction.

I wouldn't do this book and card deck justice without first saying thank you to every woman who came before me — my life has been built on your progress. To every woman in this book, your stories have enriched my life and shown me that this world is full of more possibility than I could have imagined. I feel more powerful because of you. I love myself more because of you, and for this I again say thank you.

My hope for you, the reader, is that this book and deck, the lives of these women, and the messages these pages contain inspire and empower you. May they bless your day with the wisdom you need to hear. May they guide you. May they activate any latent gifts and talents that lie dormant within you. May the trials, tribulations, and victories of these women help you overcome your greatest challenges. May they help you recognize your own power, worth, love, and honor. May they help you find your own answers and your own greatness.

Why These 44 Women?

The most challenging part of this project was choosing only 44 women out of the masses of amazing women in our world. I picked these women because they inspire greatness, courage, and love within me. All the women featured in this deck have lived relatable and relevant lives in our modern era—the 20th and 21st centuries.

There are so many more amazing women role models in the world, past and present. I have tried to represent a diverse group of ages, races, backgrounds, body types, and socioeconomic statuses in this first volume. I will continue to bring awareness and care to the women I feature in the future, and I am committed to representing even greater diversity in future volumes.

I invite you to recognize that these are real women who have lived complex and varied lives. Their lessons and wisdom come from both their greatness and their humanity. If you find that there are women in the book and deck that you have an aversion to, perhaps they have a particularly important lesson for you.

Who Is This Book & Deck For?

Everyone!

Everyone can benefit from these role models, and this book's guidance is not just for women.

Messages from Her can be used by people of all ages, though the history portion of some of the women in this book may not be age appropriate for those who haven't yet reached teenage years. If you have purchased this for a child, I recommend reading the book to them so that you can omit the more adult content, if you prefer.

How to Use This Book & Deck

You Do You
First and foremost, there are no rules. This is your book and deck to use in whatever way feels best to you. That said, there are some ways to work with this deck that I've found to be particularly useful. Below are some of my suggestions.

Card Care
When not in use, I recommend keeping your cards in their bag, box, or some other sacred and clean place. Treat these cards like a good friend, with love and care.

A note on letting other people touch your cards: Some schools of thought recommend that you don't let anyone else touch your cards. I say, do what feels best for you! Maybe sometimes you do and sometimes you don't. No need to get too serious. Try to have fun with the process.

Getting Started
Remove the cards from their special storage place. Many people like to knock three times on the top of the deck with their left hand. There are several reasons for this: Maybe it tells the ladies that you're about to ask them for some guidance; maybe it helps shift your attention to some inner knowing that will support you in picking your best card; maybe it helps clear any lingering, old energy from the cards; or maybe it's just a nice ritual. I invite you to try it or create your own ritual to prepare yourself to select a card (or cards).

Shuffle 'Em Up!

There is no exact way you need to shuffle the cards, but do shuffle them before you pull one. Shuffling helps to keep the cards fresh and allows you to change the order of whom you might pull. I personally like to shuffle my deck and then cut it in half, but there are many options.

Intention Setting

An intention can be as simple as opening up to whatever the deck or a particular woman has to teach you. I recommend taking a couple of deep breaths and seeing if a question arises. Trust that even if nothing comes to your mind or heart, your body will gravitate naturally toward the card you need at the time. Here are some examples of questions:

"What do I need to know today?"

"What aspect of my life needs healing or attention?"

"What do I need in order to feel clear about _____ decision in my life right now?"

"What quality do I need to support my happiness/relationship/ body/health/career/heart?"

There are no wrong questions, but do limit the number of times you ask the same question. Trust the answers you receive the first time, and keep yourself from pulling another card if you don't like the message.

Pick a Card, Any Card

There are many ways to choose a card. Pick from the top of the deck or within. Fan your cards or stack them straight. Arrange the cards in the way that feels best to you. Take a moment to see which card or cards you feel drawn to. Once you feel ready, pick your chosen card! Study it. What comes up for you as you look at it?

Next, refer to the book and learn the card's meaning. Take in the full guidance that the card, book, and woman have to teach you. The passages in the book contain much wisdom and guidance. If a card doesn't instantly call to you on the visual level, be sure to read the correlating meanings, paying special attention to words or sentences that stand out.

When you feel complete, either display or put your card away. Sometimes, I like to display my chosen card for the day to really anchor its meaning into my life.

Using the Book

When you pull a card, search for that woman in this book. Read her quote. Take in the passages and their meanings. Read her story. Pay attention to the information and words that stand out to you. Absorb what you read, and know that inspiration will lift off the page and travel with you throughout your day.

Feel free to use the book similarly to the deck. Set an intention or ask a question and spontaneously open any page. Sometimes, I like to travel with the book but not the cards (so they don't get damaged).

I can't recommend enough spending an extra moment learning about the women who appear in your card picks. Look at pictures of her throughout her life. Find an article about or by her. The information in this book is a sliver of her magnificence. If you regularly pick one woman, I especially suggest learning more about her; she may have more to teach you. Something in her essence and life may inspire your greatest gifts.

Card Spreads

There are so many ways to lay out and read your cards. Pull anything, from a single card every morning for daily guidance to plotting out inspiration for your whole year ahead. Get creative and make your own spread, or draw from some of my favorites here.

One & Done
Your Soul's Message
The Theme of the Day
An Answer to a Specific Question

Two-Card Spread
Stop & Go
The Problem & the Solution
Give More & Receive More
The Wound & What Will Heal It

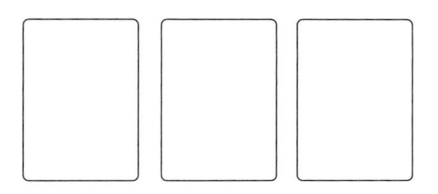

Three-Card Spread

Past, Present, Future
Embrace, Change, Let Go
Mind, Body, Spirit
Cease, Start, Continue
You, the Other Person, the Relationship

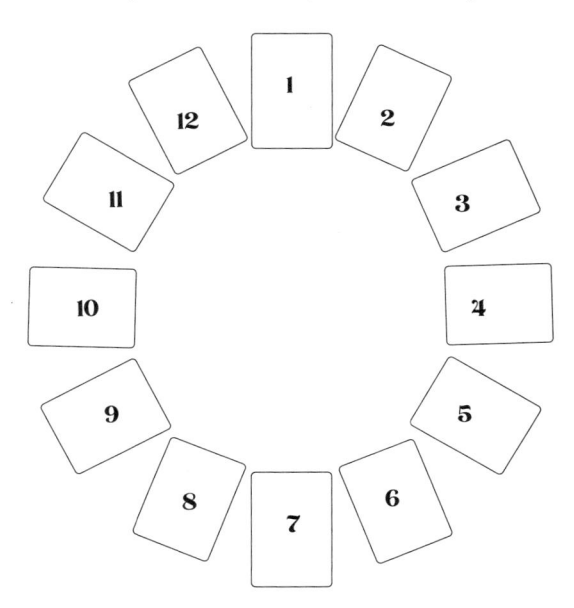

The Year Ahead

I'm a woman
Phenomenally.
Phenomenal woman,
That's me.

—Maya Angelou

The Women

Amelia Earhart
1897-1937

"Adventure is worthwhile in itself."

Meaning: ADVENTURE

Get out of your comfort zone. Change your scenery. Let yourself have an unexpected adventure. Remember that planning only goes so far, and your spirit and mind need to be regularly surprised to continue growing and evolving. You need to see things outside of your norm and everyday life to be in connection with the greater world. When you expose yourself to more of the Universe, you build greater compassion and understanding of our shared human experience. Be sure to take risks and leap into experiences of which you have no idea of the outcome.

You are also being called to question your definition of what is worthwhile and productive. Don't get caught in the idea that work is the only way to live. There are many facets to your humanity—and each is deserving of your attention.

Alternate Meaning: DREAM

Keep that head in the clouds, baby. Our dreams need no limits or boundaries. Let yourself freely hope, dream, and envision your life—your dreams give you power.

Her History

A born adventurer, Amelia spent her early years in Kansas climbing trees, capturing bugs, and building makeshift roller coasters. During a time when most girls were taught to be quiet and proper, Amelia's mother insisted she have an unconventional upbringing, encouraging her to explore her desires. Over the course of her childhood, Amelia created a scrapbook of powerful women who had broken barriers to find success in traditionally male-only professions.

During the 1918 influenza pandemic, she worked as a nurse and eventually fell ill to the disease. She was forced into a yearlong convalescence, during which she spent her time reading, learning to play the banjo, and studying mechanics. After her recovery, she had her first brush with an airplane. It whizzed by her head, and she felt it whisper something to her and her alone. Within a year, she was on her first plane ride and started working odd jobs with the sole purpose of saving $1,000 for flying lessons. She saved money and found her teacher—Anita Snook, a pioneer in female aviation. Six months later, she bought her first plane. Within a year of her first lesson, Amelia was breaking the world's distance and height flight records, but due to a series of familial financial misfortunes, she was forced to sell her airplanes (she owned several by 1922) and find traditional work. She worked as a social worker and became a member and vice president of the Boston Aeronautical Society, where she became a local celebrity for her flying skills. This led to her being chosen as the first woman to fly across the Atlantic in 1928.

After that trans-Atlantic flight, she was a household name. She began to write books about her adventures and traveled across the country to share aviation information and advocate for women's equality. She ushered in public support for passenger airlines by showing that flying was for everyone, not just daredevils. For years, she worked tirelessly to break barriers for women in aeronautics, in addition to working to change global perceptions of women and their capabilities. In 1937, Amelia Earhart mysteriously disappeared on her first circumnavigation flight around the earth but has been a treasure and mainstay in world culture ever since.

Thank you to this courageous lady of many firsts for sweeping the skies and imaginations of millions both during and after her lifetime.

Anne Frank
1929–1945

"In spite of everything, I still believe that people are really good at heart."

Meaning: HOPE

In her short-lived life, Anne Frank chose to see the good in the people and the world around her. Today, you are being asked to do the same. It can be easy to gravitate toward the dark, but, instead, choose a more loving perspective. That power lies within you. See the world through rose-colored glasses. Seeing your life this way isn't denial; it actually creates space for the best in all of us to emerge. It takes patience and dedication to perceive the world this way, but you can do it.

Speak of others with compassion and understanding. Tell people what you love about them; it will help raise them up, allowing them to become the most healed and whole versions of themselves. We all need love and understanding to transcend the problems that we face today. Can you rise above the natural human desire to judge?

Remember, recognizing the best in people doesn't mean you have to tolerate hurtful behavior. Boundaries are not separate from love. If you need to say no, say no. Rest assured knowing that the high bar you hold for yourself will inspire others to also lift their standards.

Alternate Meaning: REFLECTION

Take time to reflect on yourself and your life, even for only five minutes a day. It's time to get to know you.

Her History

Anne Frank is forever immortalized as both a beacon of innocence and hope and as a reminder of the dangers of division and hate. She was born in Germany, but her family fled the country when she was four along with the other 300,000 German Jewish citizens who fled Nazi persecution between 1933 and 1939. As the Nazis rose to power, the Frank family moved to Amsterdam, and for a while, life was good. Her father started two successful businesses, and Anne and her sister loved school. But by 1942, the Nazis had entered Amsterdam, and the family was forced into hiding in a secret annex located in one of her father's buildings. His secretary secretly fed and brought the family news of the outside world, a covert and illegal task.

Just before they went into hiding, Anne started writing in a diary, which would later become a chronicle of what it was like for so many Jewish people hiding from the Nazis during World War II. She documented those two years of her life spent in captivity with honesty. She wrote about navigating family dynamics, trying to maintain her education, and most of all about retaining a sense of hope and wonder with the world that she was locked away from. Her writing was vulnerable and helped her process the complexity of her teenage years and that time in history. Through writing, she discovered her dream of being a journalist. She felt that her love of writing was a gift from God meant to bring joy to the world. Her diary was her sustainer, the thing that left her feeling free through the difficulties of the war. In 1944, at the age of 15, Anne wrote her last entry. Just a few days later, the Nazis found the family's secret hideout and sent them off to concentration camps.

Her father's secretary gathered all of Anne's writing to return to her one day, but Anne, her sister, and her mother did not make it out of the camps. Instead, her father turned over her diary to the world to become one of the most important books of the 20th century. Anne's story is a cautionary tale against violence, destruction, and war. Her account of her own struggle humanized the struggle of the Jewish race during World War II. Anne Frank lives on as a reminder to stand for peace and compassion and to speak out against discrimination.

Blessings to this sweet girl for the lessons and hope she radiated into this world.

Annie Easley
1933-2011

"There's no age limit. You can always keep learning."

Meaning: INTELLIGENCE

This card is asking you to use your intelligence and take care of your mind. When was the last time you learned something new? Our beautiful brains need a job or a task—something to focus that power on. Make time to dive into something different. Can you think of something that's always interested you that you've pushed aside for lack of time? Explore it today!

It's never too late, and you're never too old to take up a new subject or skill. Don't expect instant perfection; let yourself be a beginner, and stick with your path. You'll catch on quicker than you think! This card especially invites you to explore STEM subjects—science, technology, engineering, and math. These subjects will work your brain, leaving it fulfilled and happily worn out. Prioritizing learning is a powerful way to keep yourself youthful, vibrant, and healthy.

Alternate Meaning: VOTE

Never let cynicism or laziness stop you from exercising your right to vote. Generations of suppressed voices gave their life to make it possible for you to vote. Honor them, the past, the present, and your future by voting!

Her History

This genius woman was born in Birmingham, Alabama, with a love of learning. Growing up in pre–Civil Rights, segregated Alabama meant that she wasn't given the same quality of education and access to resources as white children her age, but Annie was brilliant and excelled despite any limitations put on her learning. Her mother made it clear to her that she could do anything she wanted as long as she worked hard, and Annie took those words to heart. She became the valedictorian of her high school and went on to attend Xavier University of Louisiana. After graduating, she returned home to Alabama to educate other Black members of her community so that they could pass the Jim Crow–era literacy test, one of the barriers that blocked Black citizens from voting.

Shortly after her return home, she married and moved to Ohio, where she found herself temporarily unsure of her next path. This changed when she read a story in the local newspaper about a pair of twins working for the National Advisory Committee for Aeronautics (NACA, which would later become NASA) as "computers," performing math for the engineers. Magnetically drawn to the job, she applied right away. She aced the interview; two weeks later, she was working for NACA.

Annie was a remarkable mathematician, and as the technology at NASA evolved, so did she. When human computers were replaced by machines, she learned the programming language, FORTRAN, and became a programmer. She continued her education, earning her bachelor of science degree from Cleveland State University. She worked full-time and took night classes on her own dime during an era when white scientists and "computers" were sponsored by NASA to continue their education. Throughout her career, Annie dealt with subtle and less-than-subtle racism, but it never dulled her determination. She shrugged off challenges and kept going, excelling and leaving her mark on this world.

Annie worked to develop batteries for electric-powered vehicles and helped test and design NASA's nuclear reactor. She participated in the creation of the *Centaur* rocket (which put man on the moon), helped to launch the *Cassini* Saturn probe, and was a part of the team that sent NASA's *InSight* spacecraft to Mars. Annie spent over 30 years at NASA. When she finally retired, she spent her days learning new skills and mentoring others into their own greatness.

Bless this woman for her many strengths and all the ways she shared them with the world.

Aretha Franklin
1942-2018

> "We all require and want respect, man or woman, black or white. It's our basic human right."

Meaning: RESPECT

Every human you encounter is a sacred soul—a living, breathing miracle deserving of your respect and kindness. Even if you don't agree with another's views, religion, or any part of how they live their life, they still deserve your respect. There may be times when it feels hard to extend that honor, especially when we can seem so different from one another or when others are in opposition to the things we love. Listen and try to understand others. Speak and act with respect. Through these actions, you help create a world of unity.

This card also invites you to ask yourself if there are situations or people in your life who aren't showing you the kind of respect you deserve. Is there a job, relationship, or friendship that brings you down? Are you being treasured? Remember to pay attention to how sacred you treat yourself. This is how we model to others how we want to be treated. Respect yourself.

Alternate Meaning: HEARTBREAK

Heartbreak is a natural part of life. Since the dawn of humanity, no soul has avoided the pain of heartbreak. Let your heart ache; you are in a healing process. It will mend, leaving you wiser and more loving. Be gentle. Give your heart the time it needs.

Her History

This Tennessee-born icon blessed the world with soul every day of her life. Aretha's father was a preacher, and her mother was a skilled piano player and singer. From a young age, both parents infused

Aretha's life with devotion and music. By the time she was five, her father had become a pastor in Detroit, so the family moved to be with him.

Aretha sang in the choir; by age 10, she was a solo performer. She was a natural gospel singer, and by the age of 12, her father was managing her career as she traveled to perform at churches all over the country. In that first year of her career, at 12 years old, Aretha became pregnant with her first child. Aretha was focused on singing, so her grandmother and sister helped raise her child so that she could continue performing on the road.

At the age of 14, Aretha recorded and released her first gospel album and became pregnant with her second son. By her sophomore year, Aretha had dropped out of high school to perform on the gospel circuit, and by 18, she realized that she wanted to perform nonreligious music. Aretha moved with her father to New York City to jump-start her music career, and at 18 years old, Aretha signed with Columbia Records. By her early twenties, Aretha had been dubbed the undisputed Queen of Soul. She created some of the most timeless and heartfelt music ever heard, touching the world with her voice and soul.

Aretha Franklin was a powerhouse, and she undeniably carried her soulful roots into everything she did. Throughout the course of her career, she won 18 Grammys, the National Medal of Arts, and the Presidential Medal of Freedom. She was the first woman to be inducted into the Rock & Roll Hall of Fame. Aretha is remembered as one of the most skilled singers of all time, but her impact stretched far beyond music. Aretha used her fame and platform to speak up for racial equality, inspiring and empowering millions of Black people through her activism. She never performed in front of a segregated crowd in her career. Her famed hit, "Respect," by no accident became an anthem for the Civil Rights and feminist movements.

Blessings to this devoted and impassioned woman for using her voice and power to bring so much beauty, equality, and soul into the world.

Beyoncé
b. 1981

> "I don't have to prove anything to anyone. I only have to follow my heart and concentrate on what I want to say to the world. I run my world."

Meaning: POWER

Are you looking outside of yourself lately? Seeking praise? Stop distracting yourself by trying to win the approval of others or the world at large. You were born with your own inherent power, and you can reclaim it by listening deeply to the desires that lie within your heart and body. Tune in and take action on your hopes and wishes. Invest your time in living your dreams and loving yourself; this is how you create your world.

As your power grows, remember to use it wisely so that you may inspire others to reclaim their own worth and beauty. This card is reminding you to never forget that you are inherently valuable, lovable, and worthy simply because you exist. Don't give your power away by seeking validation, and don't wait for someone else to love you before you start loving yourself.

Alternate Meaning: SLAY

It's time to hustle. You've gotta grind if you wanna shine. Call upon Bey if you need some hustler energy. Only you can make your dreams come true.

Her History

This Houston-born and -raised superstar was ready to slay and inspire millions from the day she landed on this earth. From a very young age, it was evident that Beyoncé was a gifted vocalist. Her first inspiration to perform came at the age of five when she went to a Michael Jackson concert. As she watched Michael perform, she could feel it in her soul that she, too, was meant to sing, dance, perform, and entertain millions. By the age of seven, Beyoncé was winning singing contests, performing in choirs, and setting her sights on a professional singing career.

Her official career started when she was eight years old as she began singing in her first all-girls group. By the time she was 15, she was the lead singer of Destiny's Child, one of the most successful girl groups of all time. By the late '90s, Beyoncé had risen to massive fame, gaining the adoration of millions of fans worldwide. She was adored for her compelling voice as well as her powerful presence, unique beauty, and creative femininity.

By the early 2000s, Beyoncé was acting in leading Hollywood roles and branching out into her solo music career, which would prove to be one of the most innovative and dynamic careers of any musician. In the first two decades of the 2000s, Beyoncé released hit record after hit record and made the entire world her queendom, performing around the globe and back. Today, she is one of the world's bestselling music artists, having sold over 100 million records worldwide. She's received award after award for her singing, writing, producing, and performing. She's won 28 Grammys, making her the most awarded singer in Grammy history, and has the most Grammy nominations of any female artist. She is also the most awarded artist in music video history and has won the most BET awards on record. Beyoncé has repeatedly been named one of the most powerful and influential women in the world and the most powerful woman in music.

Beyoncé has achieved tremendous success as a singer, songwriter, mogul, producer, actress, icon, dancer, designer, dedicated mother, and so much more. She works every day of her life to grow, create, win, and transform into the greatest version of herself. Her presence invites and inspires millions of women to stand in their own power. She is a true and evolving creative genius, always pushing herself and pushing her creative projects to be some of the most emotional, storied, and innovative works of her time.

Bless this determined and unstoppable woman for gracing this earth with her powerful presence.

Cher
b. 1946

"All of us invent ourselves. Some of us just have more imagination than others."

Meaning: IMAGINATION

It's time to use your imagination to solve your problems. Take time to imagine the wildest, most otherworldly solutions possible. Let Cher inspire you to step into the light so people can see you for all you are and for all you aren't. This life is not about being perfect; it's about being you. Your humanity and your imperfections are what make you beautiful and relatable. Remember that you can be totally perfect in the present moment while also striving for growth and change.

In this lifetime, your success and satisfaction are tied to your ability to play with and reinvent the solidified ideas and beliefs you hold about yourself. It might be time for a rebirth. If you're afraid, ask Cher to hold your hand—she's strong enough.

Alternate Meaning: FASHION

Cher is one of the world's greatest fashion icons. Channel her ability to express herself through bold fashion. Brighten your days with the colors you choose. Cozy up or show some skin. It doesn't matter—just express who you are and where you're at with some fabulous fashion.

Her History

This goddess of youthful vigor and multifaceted talent was born in the southeastern California desert but raised all across the US. Cher was born with a natural sense of creativity and spent her early years dreaming of the day she would be famous. Throughout her youth, she held a particular fascination with the Hollywood stars of the '50s but didn't consider herself to be attractive or talented enough to follow in their footsteps. Still, this didn't quiet her soul's knowledge that fame was her destiny.

At age 16, Cher dropped out of school to study acting in Los Angeles. She was incredibly outgoing and began working at Hollywood clubs, where she would approach anyone she thought could help her reach her dreams. Her efforts paid off when she met Sonny Bono, the man who would later become both her husband as well as her producer.

Between 1962 and 1965, Sonny and Cher put out a number of experimental songs and records that were received with little enthusiasm. Despite setbacks, they continued on, and in 1965, Cher's first folk-pop album reached number 16 on the Billboard 200. In the same year, Sonny and Cher released "I Got You Babe," which reached number one on the Billboard 100 and launched them both to global fame. Cher burst onto the scene with style, glamour, and mystique — she was unlike anything the world had ever seen. Cher became equally adored for both her unique style and music.

This inventive woman triumphs wherever she applies herself. She lives as a constant creator, innovating and evolving her expression. Over the years, she's been an award-winning actress, musician, writer, comedian, businesswoman, model, television host, songwriter, record producer, fashion designer, philanthropist, and mother. There's nothing that Cher can't do. She's also one of the most epic fashion icons in the history of humanity.

Cher has been awarded a Grammy, an Emmy, an Academy Award, three Golden Globes, a Cannes Film Festival Award, the Kennedy Center Honors, and by the Council of Fashion Designers of America. She has sold 100 million records to date, becoming one of the bestselling music artists in history, and is the only artist to have a number-one single on a Billboard chart for six consecutive decades.

Here's to many more years of being graced by this woman's never-ending creativity, feminine mystique, and eternal magic.

Cyndi Lauper
b. 1953

"Girls just wanna have fun."

Meaning: PLAY

Know that this iconic '80s hit, "Girls Just Want to Have Fun," was no trite party anthem. Having fun is one of the best ways to care for yourself. Play is a fundamental human need that we tend to leave behind after childhood. Have you stopped playing in order to be taken seriously? Do you feel that the world is too heavy and that you don't deserve to play when others are struggling? Whatever your reason for not taking time for fun, your soul is calling you to consistently carve out playtime.

Integrate fun and playful moments into everything you do. Fun is an antidote to burnout, and it can revive relationships that feel flat or lifeless. Is there an area of your life that feels dull, heavy, or boring? If so, ask yourself if there is a way to play with it. You don't need an excuse to celebrate! Ask yourself: "Where do I have the most fun? What brings me the most joy?" Go there! Do that! Don't delay!

Alternate Meaning: MOODS

Your moods will change. Your energy levels will change. Your desires will change. This is all normal. A bad mood or a low moment isn't any less human or sacred than the happy ones. Let the swings come and go—it's all just part of being human.

Her History

This Brooklyn-born soul came into this world eccentric and ready to radiate. Cyndi grew up immersing herself in music, and by the age of 12, she was playing the guitar and writing lyrics. As a young girl, she stood out, dressing in bright colors and unique fashions and dyeing her hair. At the age of 17, Cyndi ran away from home to escape her abusive stepfather, landing in Vermont to study art before returning to New York City.

Cyndi spent the '70s as a lead vocalist, performing covers in numerous bands across NYC. During this time, she suffered multiple voice injuries, which forced her to take breaks from singing. She was forced into bankruptcy and had to work several odd jobs to make ends meet.

Despite Cyndi's perfect pitch, four-octave vocal range, and a singing voice that can range from childlike and innocent to deeply soulful with a rocky grit, finding her musical niche—and success—took a little over a decade. In 1983, Cyndi broke out on her own and struck gold with the release of her first solo album, *She's So Unusual*. The album peaked at number four on the charts and made her the first woman to earn four hit singles from one album. She earned a Grammy as the best new artist in 1985 and forever changed the landscape of pop music for women and global culture. Widely considered one of the best albums of the 20th century, *She's So Unusual* and its singles became anthems of their era. At the same time, Cyndi modeled a new form of feminism, characterized by playfulness, a celebration of uniqueness, and levity.

A lifelong expert experimenter, by the 2000s, she had created a top blues album as well as award-winning Broadway compositions. Her awards include Grammys, Tonys, Emmys, Billboard awards, Critics Choice awards, and much more. A phenomenal activist, Cyndi is known for supporting LGBTQ rights across the United States and through her own charities: the True Colors Fund, Forty to None Project, and the Give a Damn Campaign. A singer, songwriter, actress, activist, and mother, however she shows up, this woman brings a playful spirit, a New York City–born and –raised attitude, and a unique style to everything that she does.

Bless her and all her creations that add so much life and color to our world.

Diana, Princess of Wales
1961–1997

> "I don't go by the rule book. I lead from the heart, not the head."

Meaning: HEART FIRST

Diana had a tender and caring heart, which served as her guide in life. You are being asked to find the time to share what's in your heart with the world. Make time to support charities and those with less than you. Even if your heart feels sad or broken, giving love to others will come back to you and help heal any aches and pains. Being royal isn't all about glamour, pampering, and putting on a show—real royalty knows it's about service and heart.

Can you begin to balance logic with more heart? The heart is so powerful that it has its own electromagnetic field that envelops the entire body and is 60 times greater than the field of the brain. What do people feel as your heart radiates out into the world? Does it feel open or closed? Imagine today that people can see the energy of your heart rather than your appearance. Practice making your heart more feel-able to the world around you, and ask it to guide your words and actions.

Alternate Meaning: UPHEAVAL

Sometimes, we must leave one situation even though it grants us power or other gifts. You may be going through a painful change, but trust that miracles and opportunities exist on the other side of this disruption.

Her History

This sweet soul was born into the Spencer family of British nobility. One of five children, Diana was a shy girl who excelled in dance, sports, and music and had a naturally caring disposition. Even as a girl, her devotion to helping others was noticed by her school peers. Her childhood was unstable due to her parents' tense marriage, which ended in divorce. The pain of this was compounded by the unkind treatment she later received from her stepmother. Diana grew up in boarding schools and went to live in London when she turned 17. She took a series of jobs in those late teenage years, which included working as a children's dance instructor, hostess, cleaner, nanny, and kindergarten assistant.

Diana was 19 years old when Prince Charles began to take an interest in her. Within a year, he proposed, and only four months later, they were married. In an instant, young Diana became the Princess of Wales, the third-highest-ranking female in the United Kingdom and the most sought-after public figure in the UK. In a moment, Diana's life became constantly public.

The world instantly took Diana into their hearts. Her innocence and love shone through in the way she raised her sons, Princes William and Harry, and in the way she stepped gracefully into the public eye and charitable endeavors. She became known as the People's Princess for the down-to-earth way she lived royal life. Diana's kindness touched the world through her work to help ban land mines; protect children; and raise awareness about HIV/AIDS, cancer, and mental illness. She was also known for breaking royal traditions, from the way she raised her sons to the way she spoke up about royal life and customs.

Diana's outspokenness and refusal to conform to royal protocol created tension between her and the Royal Family, and eventually, the constant media attention put a strain on Diana's mental health and increased the stress within her marriage. In 1996, Diana and Charles divorced, but she remained a princess in the people's hearts. In 1997, Diana died in a tragic car accident. The world mourned the loss of her kind and innocent presence, but she still lives on through the memory of millions and through the impact she had on the Royal Family and the British people.

Blessings to this woman for her kindness and compassion and for showing us all how to live a heart-led life.

Dolly Parton
b. 1946

"Being a star just means that you find your own special place and you shine where you are."

Meaning: SHINE

Stop waiting for the perfect conditions to let yourself be as big, bright, happy, and magnificent as you are. You've been investing your happiness into the future, telling yourself that when you get "this," arrive "there," or find "them," happiness will be yours. Not only does waiting for the perfect conditions keep you contained and small, it also dulls your shine. You don't need to be famous to have impact, to be loved, or to be important. Here and now is as good a place and time as any to let your full radiance beam out of your every pore!

Sometimes we don't fully shine because we don't want to make others feel bad—worrying that our confidence might make another feel uncertain of themselves. Dear one, you were born to inspire. You have to let yourself shine as bright as a diamond. You've been holding yourself back from your full, brilliant expression. It's time to let it go and shine!

Alternate Meaning: CHILDHOOD LOVES

Dolly started singing before she was 10! Can you look back and remember if there was anything you loved to do as a child that you left behind when you entered adulthood? Your soul is asking you to reclaim your long-lost loves; it will nourish and heal you to do so.

Her History

What can't Dolly do? A singer, songwriter, multi-instrumentalist, humanitarian, actress, producer, super-savvy businesswoman, and international icon for more than 50 years, there's no stopping this majestic woman.

Dolly was one of 12 children raised in a one-room cabin in the Great Smoky Mountains of Tennessee, but she never let the size of that room dim her larger-than-life dreams. By the age of six, she was singing in church; seven, strumming on a homemade guitar; and 13, recording her first single. She knew where to go next. The day after she graduated from high school, she moved straight to Nashville.

Her first album, *Hello, I'm Dolly* (1967), didn't create instant stardom, but it did catch the eye of country star Porter Wagoner. He brought her on as his singing partner and featured Dolly on his hit television show. Through this collaboration, she became well-known and loved in the country music scene, but it wasn't until 1970 that she launched her own successful solo career.

It took a few years for Dolly to perfect her creative expression, but once she did, she was off to the races! Hit after hit began to pour through Dolly. She continued to develop her musical skills and build her business confidence, becoming a household name through the '70s and '80s. Dolly began to take a more active role in the production of her music and the direction of her career, becoming one of the most successful pop/country crossover artists of all time. In the '80s and '90s, Dolly was a leading lady in box office hits, opened wildly successful theme parks, and began to use her fame to support humanitarian causes, like literacy, HIV/AIDS research and treatment, and the Red Cross.

Dolly is the most successful, wealthiest, and longest-lasting country artist of all time. She has composed over 3,000 songs in her career (and still counting!), has won 10 Grammys, and has been awarded the National Medal of the Arts. She has inspired millions of people to be exactly as they are with her big hair, bigger personality, hyper-feminine style, quick-witted Dollyisms, and her consistent acceptance-of-all public messages.

Thank goodness for this one-of-a kind, illustrious wildflower of a woman.

Eleanor Roosevelt
1884–1962

"With the new day comes new strength and new thoughts."

Meaning: RENEWAL

Stop getting caught in the past, especially the stories of the past. If you have wounds that need healing, take the time to feel them and move forward into the limitless potential of your future. Whatever has come to pass no longer needs to have a hold on you. It doesn't define you. There are an infinite number of possibilities for the future of your life.

As you wake every morning, go into the world with curiosity about what gifts and opportunities the day may deliver. Ask life to bring you positive experiences that will help you grow and brighten the world around you. If you find yourself caught in negative thoughts, turn away from them. Focus on something else—something inspiring, loving, and empowering. Never underestimate the power of living in a state of wonder about the world and the people around you. Remember to ask yourself, "I wonder what will happen today?" and let life surprise you with its generosity.

Alternate Meaning: DISRUPTION

Whatever appears to be normal and fixed around you is ready to be redefined. It's time to shake things up and create new rules.

Her History

This noble woman is one of the most celebrated women in the history of the United States. Born into high society in New York City, she learned about loss at an early age, as both of her parents died when she was only a child. These deaths, and the changes they caused in her early years, impacted her for life, and she became accustomed to waves of depression. She felt out of place in high society, thinking she was too plain and practically minded. In her teens, she found her happy place in academia at a British finishing school. Upon her return to NYC, she committed to using her privilege and intellect for the good of society.

In 1905, she wed Franklin Delano Roosevelt. Her early married years were tense. She didn't take to mothering easily, though the couple had six children. Eleanor may not have been a natural in the home, but she excelled at social reform. By 1910, she was an active member of the Democratic Party, was a member of the Women's Trade League, and taught university-level history in Manhattan.

In 1933, Franklin became the 32nd president of the United States. Eleanor was nervous about being the first lady, a role that was traditionally defined as being a social hostess, but she revolutionized the role. Instead of being "seen but not heard," Eleanor became a political powerhouse, fighting for her passions: equality, education, civil rights, and the rights of women in the workplace. She traveled on FDR's behalf, attending all kinds of political events. She held press conferences for all-female reporters, who previously had not been allowed in the White House. She wrote a daily newspaper column from 1935 to 1962, producing over 8,000 entries throughout her life. She changed the idea of what women could offer the world both intellectually and politically.

After FDR's four terms, Eleanor became a UN Representative, chair of the Human Rights Committee, head of the first Presidential Commission on the Status of Women, chair on the National Association for the Advancement of Colored People (NAACP), and an advisor for the Peace Corps.

Thanks to Eleanor for spending her life creating a more equal and just society and for broadening the horizons of so many women who have come after her.

Erykah Badu
b. 1971

"If we were made in His image, then call us by our names."

Meaning: GODDESS

You are being asked to remember that you are holy. You are whole. You are the Goddess embodied. Treat yourself as such. Surround yourself with others who treat you like the divine creature that you are. Call yourself by your real name—Goddess, Queen, Magic Woman, Sacred Terrain. If you are struggling, remember your divine nature. If you are thriving, remind others of their divine nature. You have done this all before. A queen in many lifetimes, you are here to bring your distinct version of power to this planet in these changing times.

Let yourself be eccentric in your holiness. Treat your body as the temple of your soul, and know that your power comes not from your appearance but from what your soul came to this earth to share.

Alternate Meaning: WITCHY

Get witchy. It's time to believe in—and to use—some serious magic. It's available to you, and you know it. It's time to bring the mystical, the mysterious, and the enchanting into everyday life. Doing this will make you feel whole and holy.

Her History

This royal soul dropped down from the heavens with a rare version of creativity to express in this lifetime. Born and raised in Dallas, Texas, by her mother and grandmothers, Erykah was surrounded by wise women who nurtured her creative individuality. By the age of four, Erykah was already singing and dancing at the Dallas Theater Center and the Black Academy of Arts and Letters. She graduated from Booker T. Washington High School for the Performing Arts and moved to Louisiana to study theater at Grambling State University, a historically Black college. She knew that music was her path, so she left school early to focus on her writing and singing.

In the mid-'90s, her demo caught the attention of record producers, which led to the release of her first album, *Baduizm*, in early 1997. The album was met with love from both the public and critics alike. It debuted at number one on the Billboard Hip-Hop/R&B charts and number two on the overall Billboard charts. She became recognizable for her unique voice and for her ability to blend R&B, hip-hop, jazz, and soul into one of the most original sounds of the 20th century. Her experimental and empowering style of music helped popularize and define the neo-soul genre. *Baduizm* went triple platinum, won countless awards around the world, and earned Erykah her first two Grammys.

This prolific creator released her second album (and first live album) in late 1997 as she was pregnant with her first child. Titled *Live*, the album topped the charts and was certified two times platinum. Erykah took the next few years off of performing to focus on raising her son before jumping back into the music scene. Since her return, she has been creating some of the rarest music of her time.

Throughout her career, she has become known for staying true to herself, to her expression, to her heritage, and to her children. Her music unconventionally explores her African roots, motherhood, relationships, life as a Black woman in America, faith, God, and sociopolitical themes. Erykah is a mystical and magical woman who has inspired millions to live outside of norms and find their own divine paths in this lifetime.

Bless this woman for being a brilliant beacon of the sacred, self-defined, and original life.

Estée Lauder
1906-2004

> "I didn't get there by wishing for it or hoping for it but by working for it."

Meaning: WORK FOR IT

Estée Lauder may have created a brand that exudes luxury and ease, but she worked and worked to build her empire. Know that you're placing too much of an emphasis on indulgence, relaxation, and self-care. It's time to hustle to get your great work into the world. Work to become financially independent. Maybe you've never hustled before; maybe you have in the past, but it burned you out; maybe you've relied on others to get things done. None of those things matter. Just make a shift, and get out there!

If you're feeling low on motivation, call upon Estée for inspiration and help. Ask the millions of women who have come before you—women who have hustled to build their empires—to help you build yours (whether it's small or large). Do a little research about powerful women in the past who have succeeded in arenas that interest you. Let yourself learn from the achievements and mistakes of others.

Alternate Meaning: POISE

Never underestimate the power of grace and manners. Stand up straight. Be polite. Carry yourself with poise and dignity and watch how the world responds around you.

Her History

Born with endless hustle in Queens, New York, to working-class Hungarian Jewish immigrants, Estée always had her sights set on a glamorous life. She started the grind early. Her young days were spent working in her family's hardware store to help make ends meet, and in her early teens, she became fascinated by her uncle's business: a modest beauty product chemistry company. As soon as she graduated high school, she went to work for her uncle full-time and began to create her own products, like Super Rich All-Purpose Cream. She started selling to friends, the beach clubs, salons, and anywhere else she could. She loved her products and was a natural saleswoman.

Through her twenties and thirties, she continued sharpening her product formulation and business skills, all while marrying and raising two children. Estée was determined to simultaneously build her business and be a successful entrepreneur and mother, an uncommon combination of feats in the 1930s and 1940s.

Estée grew her brand by becoming a master mythmaker, adding to the allure and intrigue of her products. She would tell stories of being raised by the aristocracy in parts of Europe. She added an accent to one of the e's in her name to make it sound and appear French, and by 1946, she had established her eponymous luxury beauty brand, Estée Lauder. A marketing genius, she invented the idea of a free gift with purchase. She sold the pursuit of eternal youth and beauty, dominated the competition, and became a titan in the beauty industry.

This woman, with no formal business training, stood atop the beauty biz for all the years of her life. Her determination made her one of the wealthiest self-made women of all time. By the time Estée Lauder (company) went public in 1995, it was valued at $3 billion. She was the only woman featured in *Time* magazine's "20 Most Influential Business Geniuses of the 20th Century." That young girl who dreamt of success and elegance achieved it for herself, taught women how to live glamorously every day, and showed the world that a woman could be just as successful in business as any man.

Thanks to Estée for dreaming big, working hard, and paving the way for so many women to follow in her Business Boss footsteps.

Frida Kahlo
1907-1954

> "I am my own muse. I am the subject I know best. The subject I want to know better."

Meaning: TURN INWARD

The spirit of the artist and seeker is with you, and it knows that it can be scary to look within, as we often carry old experiences, emotions, and traumas in our body. This card is inviting you to learn that these places aren't unlovable or invaluable. Your differences and wounds hold diamonds, and they are ready to be mined.

In a world that teaches us distraction, outer pleasure seeking, and "no bad vibes," we can lose track of the beauty and complexity of our human experience. Your emotions aren't going to hurt you. In fact, facing them and feeling them is what's going to set you free. You are being asked to take the time to get to know yourself. Let outer distractions fall away.

Alternate Meaning: ROOTS

Where you come from, your family, and your lineage are all important. Are there ways that you can better understand and honor your ancestors? Whether you feel it or not, they are reaching out to support you. Learn about them. Discover your favorite qualities of your ancestors, and know those strengths also lie within you.

Her History

Born in Mexico City, Mexico, this artistic soul became an eternal icon of the global art world. While on a clear and promising trajectory to become a doctor, Frida was badly injured in a traffic accident, which left her in a full-body cast and bedridden for months. To help her kill the time and distract herself from the pain, her parents strongly encouraged her to practice her childhood hobbies of drawing and painting. Prior to her accident, she had no intention of becoming an artist, but as her activities became limited and time passed, painting became cathartic and fundamental for her expression.

Frida's body was never the same again after the accident. She experienced chronic pain for the rest of her life, but she recovered enough to return to school, where she joined the Young Communists' League. Through her connections to this group, she was exposed to many famous Mexican artists and muralists who encouraged her to continue on with her art, affirming her natural, self-taught talent.

By 1928, Frida had married the famous artist Diego Rivera. She spent the next several years of her life traveling with Diego around Mexico and the US as he painted murals. She spent this time developing and honing her art skills as well as her unique surrealist–magical style, which always incorporated aspects of Mexican folk culture, for which she had a deep love. She expressed herself and her pain—whether that was mental, physical, spiritual, or emotional—through her creativity and art in an era when women were discouraged from exposing their inner lives, details about their bodies, and their opinions. With her art, she openly explored her personal struggles with infertility and her experiences with sexuality, which she felt outside of the traditional gender and monogamy norms for the time, and she had multiple relationships with both men and women.

While her work was liked in her lifetime, leading to teaching jobs and small exhibitions, she became extremely popular after her death, in the 1970s. Her self-portraits became a symbol for the Chicano movement, the feminist movement, and the LGBTQ community. She is credited as one of the most influential Mexican artists of all time and represents the archetype of the expressive, revolutionary, and creative woman.

Bless this woman for her enduring power and presence, in both the creative and revolutionary realms of our world.

Georgia O'Keeffe
1887-1986

"Nobody sees a flower, really. It is so small, it takes time. We haven't time, and to see takes time, like to have a friend takes time."

Meaning: SLOW DOWN

You are being asked to take your time. Leave behind your expectations of speed and trust in the power of time and dedication. Most often, the very best things in life require time to fully develop and show themselves to us. Don't stop a project midstream because you lose patience. Know that there are times when you must do things you don't want to do in order to get to where you want to be. Invest in patience and consistency.

Slow down. Pay attention to the small and simple things. Let the beauty of nature nourish you and feed your senses. You were made to feel pleasure in your body, in this moment. Create opportunities throughout the day for your eyes to seek—and find—visual wonders that bring you joy. Let a slower pace of life soothe your mind and body.

Alternate Meaning: DESERT MAGIC

It's time for a cleanse, a journey, a vision quest. The seemingly barren landscape of the desert is calling you. It has something to teach you and a way to heal your body, mind, and spirit. Go to her. Don't delay!

Her History

Known as the Mother of American Modernism, Georgia O'Keeffe is one of the most well-known and influential artists of the 20th century. Born on a dairy farm in Sun Prairie, Wisconsin, Georgia was one of seven children. By the age of 10, she had made up her mind to be an artist and started taking watercolor lessons. From that point on, she never stopped learning about art, making art, teaching art, or being art.

Georgia traversed the US, learning from a host of predominant painters in the early years of her life. During this period, she taught in college art departments from South Carolina to Texas. In 1916, she caught the attention of a New York City photographer and art promoter who convinced her to eventually move to New York to focus solely on her art.

In 1929, she took her first trip to Taos, New Mexico, and fell deeply in love with its unique and otherworldly desert landscapes, hues, and shapes. In the American Southwest, she found her muse. She was enchanted, and it shone through her art. A woman who loved solitude, Georgia often explored the desert alone, traversing its landscape in her 1929 Ford Model A. This was during a time when only a small percentage of women drove, much less alone through canyons and remote wildernesses.

In the 1940s, Georgia had two retrospectives: one at the Art Institute of Chicago and another at the Manhattan Museum of Modern Art (MOMA). She was the first woman to have a retrospective at the MOMA.

Georgia O'Keeffe left a legacy of an ethereal and independent woman who shaped the terrain of abstract and landscape art for generations to come. She inspired countless women to pursue their love of art during an era when the art world focused largely on men, and she showed the world that a female artist could be just as successful and influential as a male artist. Her painting *Jimson Weed/White Flower No. 1* holds the record for the highest price paid for a painting made by a woman, selling for $44.4 million.

Many thanks to this exquisite artist for the ways in which her creativity and beauty graces this world.

Gloria Gaynor
b. 1943

"As long as I know how to love, I know I'll stay alive."

Meaning: LOVE

Let Gloria's wisdom guide you. When you feel down, focus on the love you can give, no matter if it's small or large. If your heart is broken and it feels that you may never love again, remember that romantic love is only one kind of love—you are still able to experience and share love in many different ways.

In some languages, there are many words for the different kinds of love we are capable of feeling as human beings. When one type is less strong, the others are not gone. If you center your life around giving love, you will be full of the energy you need, and the world will always bring it back to you. Can you let the purpose of your life be the giving and receiving of love? Ask love itself—that powerful energy that courses through our world—to be by your side today. Ask love to move through your actions, words, and thoughts, and then feel the way it revives you.

Alternate Meaning: MUSIC

Gloria grew up with music constantly playing in her childhood home. Fill your space with beautiful and inspiring music. It can soothe your stress, uplift dull energy, and set the tone for a romantic evening. Use music to craft the vibes of your immediate surroundings.

Her History

This New Jersey-born disco queen was steeped in music from the day she was born. Gloria's father was a musician, so records and the radio were always playing in her childhood home, and four of her five brothers formed a gospel choir. Because she was a girl, Gloria wasn't allowed to sing with the all-boys group, but she knew that, one day, she would sing. Gloria grew up in the South Side Jersey projects, poor but not without warmth. Her family kept their doors and hearts open to neighbors and filled the home with laughter and joy.

In 1961, Gloria graduated from high school and quickly sought out places and people to sing with. For 10 years, she performed in clubs up and down the East Coast, until she signed on with her first record label in 1971. In 1973, she released her first dance hits, which began to push her into the spotlight. For the next five years, she consistently kept releasing albums and performing glorious dance hits until the 1978 release of her smash hit, "I Will Survive," cemented her place in musical history. This hit earned her a Grammy and became a global anthem to the empowered single woman. At a time in history when traditional women's roles were being challenged and reshaped, the song let women know that they could stand on their own, as a single woman, with value, worth, and self-respect.

She created another hit in 1984 with the single "I Am What I Am," which the gay community quickly adopted as its empowering anthem of the '80s. Gloria used her fame to become a champion for LGBTQ rights. Musician eternal, Gloria turned to her roots in the 2000s, transitioning to gospel singing. She's been releasing records for 60 years and isn't showing any signs of slowing down.

Still rich with queenly vigor, may she continue to grace us with her vocal stylings for all her years.

Gloria Steinem
b. 1934

"A feminist is someone who recognizes the equality and full humanity of women and men."

Meaning: FEMINISM

You are being called to feminist action, but make sure that you are wielding that power wisely. Advocate for equal human rights and care for all humans in all the ways we exist in this world. Be aware of how you may blame others for creating the problems of inequity. Lasting change comes from bridging the gap of misunderstanding. Dig a little deeper into your feminism. Assess your actions, purchases, and investments in the world. Are they feminist? Do you simply talk about being feminist? Or do your actions extend to supporting organizations, schools, nonprofits, and businesses that provide equality for all those involved? Go beyond the surface, and weave your values into all aspects of your life.

Feminism is also about a sisterhood of women rising up to support each other, which includes not cutting each other down. Find ways to use your words in empowering ways that make other women around you feel loved. Stop yourself in conversations in which you speak in unkind ways about other women. Hold a high bar.

Alternate Meaning: ANGER

Anger has a bad rap, but it's a powerful ally. Listen to it. It will help you create healthy boundaries and advocate for the things you care about. Anger must move. Try yelling, boxing, or other unharmful physical releases of anger. Befriend your anger.

Her History

Born and raised in Toledo, Ohio, this American girl became a feminist powerhouse. Gloria was cued into the social injustices of women at an early age. Her grandmother was a devout suffragette who passed her knowledge and wisdom down to her granddaughter. Gloria also grew up witnessing the challenges that her mother experienced trying to find employment and medical support as a woman in the '40s and '50s. The way her mother was discounted and minimized had a profound impact on Gloria's life and in how she chose to develop and use her own power. By her teenage years, Gloria had fully realized that women didn't have the social, economic, or political equality that they deserved, and she was determined to do something about it.

Gloria pursued higher education, travel, and some short-term careers before landing her first journalism job in 1960. She wrote for *Esquire*, *Cosmopolitan*, NBC, and the *New Yorker*, covering a myriad of topics, which included a few feminist-leaning articles. In 1969, Gloria covered an abortion speak-out for the *New Yorker*. This journalistic project was the moment she felt her feminist passion, career, and advocacy begin—and she ran with it.

By 1972, Gloria had cofounded the feminist magazine *Ms*. The test print of the magazine sold out its 300,000 copies across the US in only eight days and went on to become a staple of the feminist movement.

Throughout her journalism career, Gloria has stood at the forefront of public feminist activism, gaining recognition for her writing and speaking. Over the years, her causes have grown to include environmentalism, politics, anti-war, and equality. Gloria has been granted honor after honor for her 60-plus years of advocacy and steadfastness to her work. She received an honorary degree from Yale University and numerous lifetime achievement awards and has been recognized as one of the most influential women of the 20th century. To this day, Gloria Steinem remains active in the fight for equal rights.

Thanks to this woman for consistently and passionately using her voice and words.

Helen Keller
1880-1968

"The best and most beautiful things in the world cannot be seen or even touched—they must be felt with the heart."

Meaning: FEELINGS

Helen Keller knew that our feelings have so much to tell us. There is far more to this world than the delights of your basic senses—sight, smell, touch, hearing, and taste. Are you getting carried away chasing pleasure and intense sensations and looking for answers outside of yourself? Do you feel connected to your body and instincts and all that they have to tell you? They tell us how we really feel about people, how we really want to be spending our time, and our heart's truest desires. Instead of chasing what seems or looks good, can you chase what feels good—deeply, wholeheartedly good—not a fleeting, momentary desire?

Remember, the world is delivering little miracles and bursts of love to you throughout all your days. Can you receive more? Can you watch for all the ways beauty shows up for you: a smile from a stranger, a kind word, a gentle breeze, a heavy blanket? The world is giving and giving, and you are being called to feel its blessings.

Alternate Meaning: NOTHING IS IMPOSSIBLE

This is a reminder that whatever seems or feels impossible, impassable, or stuck in your life right now is not. It is temporary. Hold the vision of a miraculous shift in your mind and heart. It will come.

Her History

This queen of miracles was born in Tuscumbia, Alabama, as a healthy baby girl with full senses, but at 19 months, she fell ill, leaving her both deaf and blind. This didn't stop Helen. She was a brilliant and determined child with a particularly resilient spirit. By the time she was seven, she had invented over 60 communication signs and could recognize people in her home by the vibration of their footsteps. Her parents were determined that she would live a happy and normal life, so they sought out schools and doctors that specialized in the emerging field of working with the deaf.

After many trips to the northern United States, they found the Perkins Institute for the Blind, where the school's director recommended that they hire Ann Sullivan, a former student, to educate and care for Helen. On March 5, 1887, Ann Sullivan arrived to take her lifelong place by Helen's side. Helen called that day her soul's birthday. Within a month, she was learning rapidly, and in a little over a year, she was fluent enough in both signing and communication that she was able to attend Perkins Institute for the Blind herself. Ann stayed on with her throughout her entire education—which took her to Radcliffe and then to Harvard University, where she became the first deaf and blind person to earn a bachelor's degree.

In time, Helen learned how to speak and became an excellent writer. She spent her life traveling the world, becoming a lecturer, author, and activist for disabled people's equal rights, women's suffrage, labor rights, and anti-militarism. During her lifetime, she wrote 14 books and 500 articles, spoke in over 35 countries, and impacted countless policies, including the adoption of braille as the writing and communication system for the blind. She became known for her inspiring and positive attitude, spreading messages of hope and her anything-is-possible attitude throughout the globe.

Against the greatest odds, Helen Keller created miracle after miracle throughout her life. Blessings to this woman and her heartfelt determination, which enhanced the lives of so many who came after her.

Irena Sendler
1910-2008

> "Heroes do extraordinary things. What I did was not an extraordinary thing. It was normal."

Meaning: IMPACT

You don't need superpowers or millions of dollars to make a change in this world—we are all capable of having a powerful impact on the lives of others. You are being called to give without the expectation of receiving anything in return. Remember that to care for each other is a basic human capability. How can you help stand against injustice, violence, and harm in this world? And can you do it without the motivation of being seen as an altruistic, heroic, or saintly person?

What would you do if there was no reward? How would you behave if no one could see your actions? Don't let the glamour of heroism drive you. You have the opportunity to protect those with less privilege than you. The resources you have access to in this lifetime are here for you to share with others. Extend a helping hand today.

Alternate Meaning: CHILDREN

Tune into the purity, play, and sanctity of children. They represent new life and endless possibilities. Do what you can to love and support the children around you and in the world at large.

Her History

Irena Sendler touched countless lives with her care. She was raised outside of Warsaw, Poland, in a Roman Catholic family that believed in the fair treatment of all humans. Her father was a doctor who offered free treatments to all of his patients, including Polish Jews, who faced much anti-Semitism at the time. In college, Irena was known for speaking out against the unequal treatment of Jewish students and citizens in Warsaw.

In the 1930s, Irena joined the Union of Polish Democratic Youth and the Polish Socialist Party—both groups opposed anti-Semitism, the Nazis, and World War II. By this time, she had become a social worker. She focused on helping children born out of wedlock and their single mothers.

By 1939, the Nazis invaded Poland and created the Warsaw Ghetto, the largest of all the Jewish ghettos in German-occupied Europe. Over 400,000 Jewish men, women, and children were held in the ghetto, where they had little to no access to basic necessities. Irena used the Nazi's fear of typhoid fever to obtain permits to enter the ghetto with the facade of inspecting homes to spot the disease. Her "inspections" began by her smuggling in clothing, food, and medicines, but she saw the grim fate for the citizens of the ghetto and began to sneak children out as quickly as she could.

Between 1940 and 1943, Irena snuck out thousands of Jewish children. She created networks of hiding places and kept records of all of their names, families, new Christian names, and locations, so that they could one day be reunited with their families. She became a crucial operator in Zegota, an underground anti-Nazi group that helped place children in safe homes.

In 1943, Irena was arrested by the Gestapo. She was tortured for a month before being ordered to death. Despite the brutal treatment, she never gave up anyone whom she had helped or had worked with. On the way to execution, she was released by a guard who had been bribed by Zegota to save her.

During the remainder of WWII, she hid as a hospital nurse outside Warsaw, still supporting Zegota from a distance. To the very end of her life, Irena dedicated herself to social work, nursing, and education. In her later life and after her death, she was recognized globally for saving over 2,500 children in the years that she ran the Zegota children's network.

Many thanks to this woman for her courageous heart and unwavering strength.

Jane Addams
1860-1935

> "The good we secure for ourselves is precarious and uncertain until it is secured for all of us and incorporated into our common life."

Meaning: EQUALITY

You are being called to social justice work. Know that no matter how successful you are, if it comes at the expense of another, it isn't sustainable or a real achievement. Your comfort and care need not come at the detriment of others. Use your power wisely. Seek out businesses and causes that give back to the less fortunate. Work to integrate these businesses into your daily life, actions, and purchasing habits.

This card is especially calling you to care for the children of this world. You are being called to become an advocate for their well-being. Donate school supplies, volunteer, or seek out opportunities to bring more equality into the lives of children. It is your work to make sure they are afforded equal opportunities, for they were innocently born into a world that lacks equality. They all have unlimited potential, and you can help them on the path toward living their greatest lives.

Alternate Meaning: POVERTY

Never look down on those with less than you. The poverty that others experience isn't about them but rather highlights our societal and political systems that are designed to keep people poor. Break down your prejudices or discomfort around those who exist in poverty.

Her History

Jane was born to be a reformer, with a heart set on securing the welfare of all humans. Born into a wealthy family in Illinois, she was expected to follow the standard path for well-off women of her era, but she created her own.

Jane's mother died when she was only two, leaving her to be raised by her two sisters. Jane always felt out of place in high society and had no wishes to be married, start a family, or organize social functions. She knew that her calling was to be of service, but she wasn't yet sure of how this path would take form. This uncertainty left her depressed and purposeless through her twenties until she discovered the Reformist Social Movement—a new group forming in London. The movement brought the rich and poor together through physical proximity and resource sharing, which in turn created compassion, uplifting, and a breakdown of the barriers between classes.

In 1889, using her own money, Jane established Hull House in a run-down mansion in an immigrant neighborhood of Chicago. Hull House grew into a 13-building complex, supported by many wealthy local families. It contained a medical center, after-school clubs, night classes for adults, a public kitchen, a gym, an art gallery, a girls' club, a bathhouse, a theater, a library, meeting rooms, and apartments. It became a research hub for local issues like truancy, childbirth, food shortages, children's health care, prostitution, and education. These studies and related services birthed modern social work and were adopted as the national model for social care.

As an activist, social worker, sociologist, and author, Jane traveled the world promoting equality for all. She championed global peace and women's suffrage, causes for which she was awarded the 1931 Nobel Peace Prize, making her the prize's first American female recipient. She was the first woman to receive an honorary degree at Yale and the first publicly recognized female philosopher in the US. She cofounded the American Civil Liberties Union (ACLU) and became a role model for women on how to empower themselves to change their local communities and the world at large. When she passed away in 1935, she was one of the most well-known and respected public figures in the US. Jane Addams forever changed how we care for each other and how the government cares for its people.

Bless this pioneering woman for all of her society-sculpting work and inspirational leadership.

Jane Goodall
b. 1934

"The least I can do is speak out for those who cannot speak for themselves."

Meaning: ANIMAL LOVE

You have a special connection with animals. Animals are here to teach us the many ways to live on this earth and to help us discover more unconditional love. Your animal connection nourishes and supports you. You can easily communicate with and comfort them. Be inspired to spend more time with animals. Be present with them. Talk to them. Let them love you, and love them in return. Advocate for their wellness, and find animal care groups to support. It will do your heart and body good, as well as theirs.

Remember, we are also animals. We have our own reptilian brains and animal physiology that creates contractions, reactions, and feelings of fleeing, fighting, or freezing. Understanding your animal nature can help you have more compassion for yourself when you feel afraid, triggered, or upset. We're all animals trying to figure out this big world and our complex experiences. Treat yourself with the same care and kindness you would show your favorite baby creature.

Alternate Meaning: BODY LANGUAGE

We humans can get very caught up in the words we use. It's time for you to instead focus on your body language. What is it communicating to the outside world? What is your body saying to others, but more importantly, what is it saying to you? Where, when, and with whom does your body contract, and when does it open? Pay attention. Your body language is just as important as your verbal language.

Her History

This kind woman was born to care for the fauna of this world. Raised in England, Jane began dreaming of faraway lands and animals at an early age. When she was a year old, her father gave her a stuffed chimpanzee, which began her love affair with animals. She expressed her desire to live in Africa to her mother, who encouraged her to pursue her dreams.

Jane didn't have enough money to attend college, so she got a secretarial job at Oxford University while still dreaming of living in Africa. In 1956, destiny intervened when a friend invited Jane to join her family at their farm in Kenya. Jane immediately began saving money for the boat ride, and by the age of 23, she arrived in Kenya, where she met the famous archaeologist and paleontologist Louis Leakey. Impressed with her knowledge of Africa and its animals, he hired Jane as his assistant.

By 1960, Jane was studying chimpanzees in Tanzania, but her mother had to accompany her, as the British government wouldn't approve of a woman living alone in the jungle. With the patience of a saint, Jane spent five years lovingly gaining the trust of the chimpanzees, which allowed her to make some of the most impactful primate discoveries in the history of animal behavior science. In 1962, Louis Leakey organized funding and permission for Jane to earn her PhD at the University of Cambridge. Upon graduation, she returned to her two great loves: Africa and its animals.

Jane is the most well-known conservationist and animal rights advocate across the globe and is the world's leading expert on chimpanzees. She taught the world that animals have far more intelligence and feelings than we imagined. Her work ushered in a new wave of thought around the internal—and previously unconsidered—lives of animals. She has inspired others to conserve and live in harmony with the natural world and has empowered countless women to break into the historically male-dominated studies of primatology and conservation, helping to bring much more equality to those scientific fields.

Thanks to this sweet woman for her tireless service to the gentle creatures of this world.

Janelle Monáe
b. 1985

> "Even if it makes others uncomfortable, I will love who I am."

Meaning: SELF-LOVE

Self-love is an act of rebellion. This world teaches us to only fully love ourselves when others love us, when we fit the mold of what society likes to see, when we're fit enough, smart enough, soft enough, successful enough (but not too successful!), young enough, old enough, educated enough, photogenic enough, rich enough (the list goes on!). Choosing to love oneself in the face of all these messages is a genuine revolution. Don't let anyone or anything distort your true value or beauty. Love yourself fiercely.

Look around you. Are you working too hard to make others comfortable? Do you find yourself in constant agreement with your friends and family? It might be a sign that you are living for others, rather than fully expressing yourself. Look for opportunities to express yourself. Your desires matter. If self-love feels like a challenge, make a practice of writing down one thing you love about yourself every night before you go to bed. It might make you uncomfortable at first, but it will be well worth it.

Alternate Meaning: SEE BEYOND

Don't get caught up in appearances. There is something about everyone and everything to love and value on this earth. It's time for you to transcend the emphasis you place on the limited range of what pleases you visually.

Her History

Janelle came into this world with a unique soul and a voice made for expression. She was raised in a working-class community in Kansas City,

Kansas, where she first found her voice singing in church. Janelle was born with a vivid mind, which helped her to rise above the challenges of her surroundings. She began creating her own brilliant internal worlds—a talent she would infuse into all her future works. With creativity in her bones, Janelle wrote her first musical by the age of 12.

After high school, she moved to New York City to study music and performance but felt confined playing defined roles. She knew there was a better place for her, so she left New York for Atlanta to attend Georgia State University. There, she was able to explore more of herself—what wanted to be written through her, sung through her, and performed in new ways. She soon caught the eye of famous musicians and record labels that were easily able to see her unique style. When she was signed to Bad Boy Records, the label knew they just had to expose her to a wider audience and she would create her own gravitational pull. Her imaginative stylings, inventive lyrics, impeccable fashion sense, and futuristic videos quickly garnered her national attention.

Janelle has become a favorite of both critics and fans. She is one of the world's most innovative artists and also a fierce and creative advocate for issues of race, inequality, LGBTQ rights, and feminism. She is a vocal supporter of minorities and anyone who feels separate or marginalized. She deeply questions the norms of society, including the norms of her own identity, sexuality, and gender. She identifies as a woman but also nonbinary beyond her womanness, as well as pansexual, having the ability and desire to love and be attracted to anyone based on who they are rather than what gender they identify as.

Janelle has released three studio albums, four EPs, 20 singles, one published book, and 18 music videos, all while sharpening her acting skills in powerful film roles. In 2014, she was awarded the Harvard Women's Center Award for Achievement in Arts and Media as an artist and advocate.

Blessings to this prolific human as she keeps evolving, creating, and supporting the world around her with every passing year.

Julia Child
1912-2004

"Find something you're passionate about and keep tremendously interested in it."

Meaning: PASSION

At any time, at any age, and at any phase of life, you are absolutely able to take on an entirely new interest, hobby, or passion—and it doesn't need to make sense! Whatever your heart feels called to do, do that. Whatever piques your curiosity, that's the direction to go in. You aren't simply being encouraged to do something new; you are being ordered to! Learning new things brightens the soul and keeps you young. It literally creates new gray matter in your brain, which keeps it from shrinking. Think of learning new and novel things as your insurance policy for graceful aging.

As you learn something new, you will find new loves along the way—new parts of yourself you haven't met yet, new people from your new activities, and new aspects of life that you have yet to experience. The world is a never-ending playground of fascination. Try something new, and get out of your comfort zone. Give it your all, and then do it all over again!

Alternate Meaning: LOVE THY FOOD

You need to develop a healthy and loving relationship with the food you eat. Love it, appreciate it, and take time to value all the people and the nature that brought it to you. Let the meals you prepare be your heart's creation and your body's medicine.

Her History

This cheerful California-born star would grow up to be the greatest cooking icon in the United States, though nothing in Julia's early life hinted at her future in the culinary arts. Her schooling was typical, and she spent her free time pursuing athletic hobbies. In her college years, she earned a history degree from Smith College in Massachusetts.

When World War II began, Julia tried to enlist in the Women's Army Corps, but they refused her because, at six feet two inches, she was too tall. Instead, she was accepted at the OSS (Office of Secret Services) and worked for years in Washington, DC, and Sri Lanka as a top-secret researcher. It was in Sri Lanka that she met her husband, Paul Child.

Paul introduced Julia to French cuisine, and after one life-changing meal in France, she became infatuated with mastering the art of cooking. Though she was known to be a terrible cook well into her 30s, that one divine dining experience opened something in her soul. She quickly enrolled at the most prestigious culinary school in Paris, Le Cordon Bleu. A determined creature, she then apprenticed with some of the most famous French chefs in Paris. For the next 10 years, she taught others all over Europe how to cook.

When she moved back to the US, she collaborated on the bestselling 726-page cookbook *Mastering the Art of French Cooking*. The book was a marvelous success and led to Julia's first cooking show, in 1963. Julia wasn't the first TV chef, but she quickly became one of the most adored TV personalities, hosting some of the greatest cooking shows of all time. She was the first woman inducted into the Culinary Institute of America's Hall of Fame and showed the world that women, as well as men, could be professional chefs.

Julia's impact reached beyond the kitchen. Due to the technology of the '60s, her shows were unedited, which revealed her mistakes, jokes, and humanity in a time when the expectations were high for women to be proper, infallible, impeccably clean, and perfect housewives. With her genuine and cheerful nature, she helped millions of women feel more comfortable being human.

Thanks to this boisterous and sunny woman for sharing her love and curiosity-filled life so generously with the world.

Julia Louis-Dreyfus
b. 1961

"I have no agenda except to be funny."

Meaning: LAUGHTER

You need a good laugh. Your mind and body are calling for it, and laughter is an elixir of health. It lowers stress hormones, raises immune cells, and produces infection-fighting antibodies, all of which support a healthy immune response. Laughter also triggers a release of endorphins. Endorphins are your "happy" neurotransmitters that reduce the brain's pain receptors, modulate appetite, and release sex hormones. Studies have shown that laughter decreases blood pressure and improves cardiovascular and heart health. Laughter also reduces bouts of anxiety and depression.

Don't forget to laugh with others too! Laughter evolved in humans as a way of communicating genuine care and safety. Build goodwill by spending quality time laughing with your friends. Socialize, let yourself be amused, and definitely don't be too cool to lose yourself in laughter.

Alternate Meaning: CITY & CULTURE

Your soul and mind need you to spend more time in the heart of the city. Seek out art, different kinds of food, people, and diverse thought leaders. Expose yourself to all that the vibrant city and its culture has to offer.

Her History

This leading lady loves to make people laugh. A natural-born comedian, Julia Louis-Dreyfus is one of the most successful and awarded television actors of all time.

Julia was born in New York City but moved to Washington, DC, when she was four. By the time she was ready to go to college, she landed at Northwestern University in Illinois, where she studied theater. She was clear on her path to become a performer and a star, so she dropped out of Northwestern at 21 when she landed a spot on *Saturday Night Live*. At the time, she was the youngest female cast member to ever be hired to the show. She made the most of her time there, practicing her craft and making connections. After performing on *SNL* for three years, she moved on to other sitcom projects. In 1989, Julia landed the role of Elaine Benes in a new series, *Seinfeld*, and the rest is comedic history. Her portrayal of Elaine earned her fame, adoration, and award after award.

Later in her career, Julia became known for taking more creative control and production credit in the projects she worked on, which was an uphill battle in the male-dominated comedy and television industries of the '90s. Julia ushered in and inspired an entirely new wave of female comedians, opening the door for the scores of funny ladies who came on the scenes in the early 2000s.

Post-*Seinfeld*, Julia has created hit after hit, going on to star in many other sitcoms and movies. In her career, she has won five American Comedy Awards, 11 Emmys, nine SAG Awards, two Critics' Choice Awards, one Golden Globe, and one TV Critics Association Award. She has been inducted into the TV Hall of Fame, has a star on the Hollywood Walk of Fame, and was awarded the nation's highest comedy honor, the Mark Twain Prize for American Humor, presented by the Kennedy Center.

Throughout her career, Julia has lovingly balanced motherhood, marriage, and her personal life with fame. She's a breast cancer survivor and publicly advocates for environmental health, sustainability, equality, and universal health care.

Here's to decades more of laughter and levity from this goddess of comedy.

Lizzo

b. 1988

> "Yeah I got boy problems
> that's the human in me.
> Bling bling then I solve 'em
> that's the goddess in me."

Meaning: TRANSCEND

Lizzo's no fool. She knows that, no matter where she's at or what she's got going on, she's a goddess through and through. She knows that she's half human, half divine — and we need both parts to thrive in this world. Know that the current problems you face and the current wishes you have can't be solved by your human mind. Lift your desires up to a higher power, God, Goddess, or the divine parts of you that can see your life from a higher perspective. Once you do, let them go! Trying to constantly figure things out with your mind is a drain on your precious energy. Thank that beautiful brain for functioning and supporting your life, and let it know that, for now, it's not the right tool for the job. It's time for your divine essence to take the wheel.

The more you use your queenly powers, the stronger they'll become. Problems will become easier and easier to solve. Remember: Lift those desires and challenges up to a higher power! If they're meant for you, they'll come around, and if they aren't, something far greater will take their place.

Alternate Meaning: TWERK

Your body was meant to gyrate and move! You were born into this world with a need to dance. Dancing improves your mental, physical, spiritual, and emotional health and helps you release things that are no longer serving you. Twerk it out!

Her History

An unstoppable force, this musical maven had her sights set on performing and sharing her unique vocal creations from her early childhood days. Detroit born and Houston raised, Lizzo was rapping by the age of 10 and performing in her first band, Cornrow Clique, by the age of 14. Lizzo has always been a lady of diverse interests, and in college, she studied classical music, specializing in flute, and performed in the marching band in an effort to bring balance to both her musical and performance skills.

A musical love child of hip-hop, soul, R&B, and classical flute, Lizzo has birthed some of the rarest and funkiest hits of her day—and she's always worked hard for her success. She spent a year living in her car, working her way up the low-paying, late-night gig ladder to build her name recognition. Lizzo released a number of amazing albums between 2013 and 2019, but it was her 2019 record drop, *Cuz I Love You*, that launched her into overnight stardom and won her her first three Grammys. She quickly became a pop queen and cultural icon as her fame spread like wildfire in the months following the record's release. She went on to win Billboard Awards, BET Awards, People's Choices Awards, and more. In 2022, Lizzo released her fourth studio album, *Special*. The lead single from the album, "About Damn Time," reached number one on the Billboard top 100, landed Lizzo in the top 10 in 12 other countries, and won her a Grammy for record of the year.

Lizzo uses her powerful and purposeful voice both in and out of the musical realm. She's a phenomenal advocate for self-love, body positivity, racial and gender equality, LGBTQ rights, and mental health. She inspires her wide range of fans to care for themselves, value their worth, and love themselves exactly as they are. This Grammy-winning queen is just getting started and is sure to gift the world with her uplifting and vivacious wisdom for all of her days.

Big thanks to Lizzo for gracing us with her rare and beautiful presence on this earth.

Madonna
b. 1958

"I am my own experiment. I am my own work of art."

Meaning: TRAILBLAZER

Don't let the small ways that society has defined art and creativity confine you. Your life is your canvas, and no one holds a patent on creativity and expression. You are being asked to go your own way, to change your style, your opinions, your needs, your jobs, your home, and anything else in your life that needs a shake-up. Do this as many times as you want or need—you don't need anyone else to lead the way or to show you what's possible. Break the rules. Bend the norms. Defy convention. Pay attention to random creative urges, and let them unfold as an experiment while remaining unattached to the outcome.

Never let anyone else's ideas about life, expression, or sexuality define you. You are an innovative artist. You were born to create your own path. This life is your own beautiful adventure. You can play with it, rewrite it, scrap it, and restart it as many times as you want. There are no rules.

Alternate Meaning: SEX & SENSUALITY

Your sexuality and sensuality are both important parts of your humanity. Experiment with them and pay attention to all the things that you can do to bring yourself pleasure.

Her History

This extraordinary woman was born and raised in Michigan in a large Catholic Italian family. Her home was full of Catholic iconography, she attended church and Catholic school, and her mother often had priests and nuns over to the house. At the age of five, Madonna's mother died of cancer, which had a great impact on her. She rebelled against home life, social norms, and Catholicism, but she was also a perfectionist who excelled academically, graduating high school early and earning a dance scholarship to the University of Michigan.

At the age of 20, Madonna left college to study dance in New York City. The move took courage. She had never been on a plane or in a taxi, and she only had $35 to her name. She worked as a waitress while studying with dance legends Martha Graham and Pearl Lang. One year later, she was working as a professional backup dancer. In 1982, she began to experiment with music and released her first two hit singles. In 1983, she created her eponymous hit record, *Madonna*, and has been a global superstar ever since. By the time she released her second album, *Like a Virgin*, she was officially the Queen of Pop. *Like a Virgin* became the first female album to sell over 5 million copies.

Madonna's music skyrocketed her to stardom, but her personality became equally impactful and magnetic. She set the bar for fashion trends in the '80s and '90s and redefined what it meant to be a female artist in the music industry. She became known for her overt sexuality, outspokenness, addictive performances, and record-breaking career. Through example, Madonna set free the creative and sexual expression of millions of women around the world. Before Madonna, mega-superstar musicians and singers were primarily men. Madonna broke into the boys' club and erased boundaries like none other, paving the way for all the female artists who have come after her.

An activist, humanitarian, actress, singer, songwriter, fashion icon, designer, record producer, dancer, author, director, and mother—Madonna can do it all. Madonna is the bestselling female recording artist of all time, and she's still got more records coming. This woman stands the test of time, re-creating and innovating herself whenever and however she wants.

Many thanks to this innovative woman and her society-transforming creative genius.

Malala
b. 1997

"I am stronger than fear."

Meaning: COURAGE

Know that you are stronger than you think. No internal fear or external foe will ever keep you down. You are made of golden valor and courageous matter through and through. There may be times in life when you feel defeated or like you can't make it through, but have faith. Give yourself a moment (or as many moments as you need!) to rest, then get back up and try again. Expect success and a positive outcome. With every doubt, test, or drama that you triumph over, you build your own confidence and learn that you are your own hero, your own knight in shining armor.

Fears are temporary. They may feel eternal, but trust in the changing nature of life, and know that with your bravery, dedication, and intelligence, you can achieve anything. As you embody bravery and courage in this world, you teach others to do the same.

Alternate Meaning: USE YOUR VOICE

You've got a voice. What do you think it was meant for? Use it! Speak up for yourself! Speak up for what you believe in! Use that powerful voice whenever you can!

Her History

Malala was born with a thirst for knowledge and equality. At the young age of 11, she was writing a blog for the BBC about the oppression and occupation of the Taliban in her home in the Swat District in Khyber Pakhtunkhwa, Pakistan. She was educated by her father, who was a school owner, an educational activist, and a poet. He could see at an early age that Malala was remarkably wise, and he encouraged her to pursue politics and activism.

When the Taliban began to ban music, television, and girls' education by blowing up all-girls schools, Malala revolted through journalism. Dangerous as it was, she handwrote notes that reported the daily living conditions of a young girl in a war zone, passing them along to a journalist who got them back to the BBC. At the end of her assignment for the BBC, the *New York Times* made a documentary about her, making her a prominent voice against the Taliban and the injustices facing the Pakistani people. The documentary led to more interviews and writing, making Malala a public figure across the globe.

The more Malala courageously spoke out against the destruction and cruelty of the Taliban, the more dangerous her life became. At the age of 15, a Taliban gunman attempted to murder Malala and forever silence her voice. It took months for Malala to recover, but when she did, her voice was clearer and more confident than before. An outpouring of love rose from across the world to support Malala's recovery and her foundation, The Malala Fund. The Malala Fund is a global organization that gives girls access to education and leadership opportunities in parts of the world where opportunities are denied or limited.

Upon her recovery, Malala coauthored *I Am Malala*, which made her a bestselling author at the age of 16. At 17 years old, she was awarded a Nobel Peace Prize for her work to bring education and freedom to children across the globe, making her the world's youngest Nobel Laureate.

Bless this brave young woman and her voice, which she uses to boldly advance the safety and opportunities of so many others.

Marie Curie
1867-1934

> "Nothing in life is to be feared, it is only to be understood. Now is the time to understand more, so that we may fear less."

Meaning: KNOWLEDGE

Fear is a normal part of being human, but don't let it control your actions. When you are afraid of something, someone, or a group of people, very often this fear comes from a lack of understanding. It's natural to fear what we don't know—we're wired this way. But we're also wired for connection, compassion, and learning. Is there something or someone you don't understand? Take the time to learn and grow. Expand your knowledge.

Remember to use your mental body to its fullest capacity. Consume information like breakfast. Challenge your ideas. Be humble enough to ask questions, for intelligence is not about knowing everything; it's about being honest when you don't know something. As you learn and gain wisdom, others will turn to you for leadership and teaching. Remember to share what you learn for the betterment of everyone.

Alternate Meaning: PRACTICE

Marie Curie wouldn't have gotten anywhere without a lot of experimentation in her labs. Everything takes practice. Give yourself the time and space to master what's important to you. Don't expect overnight perfection.

Her History

The day this brilliant creature was born, she set out on her path to forever change the world.

Marie was born in Russian-occupied Poland into a family full of teachers. When the Russians shut down her father's science lab, he brought it home to teach his children how to use every instrument. Still, education wasn't easy to come by as a woman, or as a Polish citizen, due to the restrictive Russian curriculum and censorship. By her teens, Marie had begun to attend Flying University, a secret college created to give Polish youths access to a good education.

An insatiable learner, at age 24, she went to France to study physics, chemistry, and math at the University of Paris. It was a meager life, but her love of learning sustained her. In 1893, she earned her first degree in physics. A year later, Pierre Curie, a fellow scientist, opened his lab to her. Their shared love of science quickly drew them together, and by 1895, they were married. Marie spent her time mothering, teaching (as the first female teacher at Paris's most prestigious graduate school), and researching uranium for her PhD. Pierre, so taken by her work, dropped his own studies to join her. In 1898, they published their discoveries of radium and polonium and coined the term "radioactivity." In the next five years, they published over 30 studies that proved tumor-forming cells were destroyed faster than healthy cells when exposed to radium, one of the most significant scientific discoveries in history.

In 1903, Marie received her PhD and a Nobel Prize in physics, making her the first woman ever to receive the award. By 1910, she had successfully isolated radium and won a second Nobel Prize, this time in chemistry, making her the first person—and only woman—to win two Nobel prizes. In World War I, she used her genius for the greatest good by creating mobile X-ray units, which were used to treat over 1 million soldiers on the battlefront. She went on to establish world-class research labs across Europe that have eternally impacted the course of science. She toured the globe, inspiring millions of women to become active in the sciences.

In 1934, Marie Curie passed away, leaving a legacy as a true global science icon and one of the greatest geniuses that the world has ever seen.

The most enormous thanks to this history-altering, scientific maven.

Marie Forleo
b. 1975

> "There has never been and never will be another you. You have a purpose—a very special gift that only you can bring to the world."

Meaning: INDIVIDUALITY

Marie could tell you without a shadow of a doubt that you are unique. Your message is important for you to express and for the world to hear. Sometimes, it's easy to feel like everyone else is unique or creative and that you weren't given the same stuff that they're made of. This simply isn't true. You, exactly as you are, have never existed in the history of the world. You could spend your life searching the globe for someone exactly like you, and you'd never find them. Whatever you have to say, create, or express, do it and stop worrying about how it's going to turn out. It doesn't matter if it's been done before—it's never been done the way that you're going to do it.

Remember that nothing happens without determination, dedication, and discipline. Try and try again. A child doesn't fall a few times and give up on walking. They fall as many times as they need to master their new and crucial skill. Don't interpret mistakes or challenges as your inability to do something. Get in it to win it. Trust yourself, and remember there is no one else exactly like you.

Alternate Meaning: ACTION

Marie was right on when she said, "Clarity comes from action, not thought." Test things out! Try things on! Don't live in your imagination. Get out there into the real world, and just do it!

Her History

This inspirational Jersey girl spreads light, lessons, and play wherever she goes. An author, dancer, inspirational speaker, business-savvy boss, teacher, and life coach to millions around the globe, Marie Forleo is a woman of action who transforms dreams into reality. She spent her early career days on the New York Stock Exchange trading floor, only to realize she had many passions and curiosities besides the NYSE, none of which she was willing to leave behind. She moved into advertising and editing in the stylish worlds of *Gourmet* and *Mademoiselle* magazines, then on to hip-hop choreography and dancing for MTV and Nike.

She continued to joyfully experiment in all the realms of her diverse curiosities, landing next in a coaching program while bartending long nights on the side so that she could build up her new clientele. Marie quickly fell in love with supporting other people in the pursuit of their dreams. Shortly after she established her coaching practice, she transformed it into a digital empire, with an online TV program with over 52 million views, an online business school for entrepreneurs, newsletters, and inspirational interviews. She teaches millions of people how to access their greatest dreams and then turn those dreams into reality and a more brilliant and profitable life than they ever imagined possible.

A thought leader and visionary, Marie became a *New York Times* number one bestseller with the release of her motivating book *Everything is Figureoutable*.

Marie stands as an eternal optimist, reminding humanity that the world needs us exactly as we are. She tells us that we are infinitely more powerful than we believe and that there is no predetermined or right way to live. She's living a life that she loves and sharing how to do it with as many people as possible in her lifetime.

Thanks to this shining star for all her hard work and hustle that so greatly benefits us all.

Marilyn Monroe
1926-1962

"It's all make believe, isn't it?"

Meaning: CHARISMA

Marilyn knew the power of personas and playing with the full range of human expressions. She knew that charisma could be developed, just like any other skill. It's time to practice being more open, engaged, and expressive. The most charismatic people are the ones who make others feel amazing about themselves. Build your charisma by uplifting, listening to, and complimenting others. Your personality is not fixed; you can pick up desirable qualities and drop undesirable ones whenever you want. Be careful about the hardened beliefs you have about yourself and others. Unexamined, these ideas can confine your life and your capabilities. Remember that we're all making it up as we go!

Marilyn also knew that no human is meant to be "on" all the time. Being constantly engaged can burn you out and drain your precious energy. Learn when to give and when to hold back.

Alternate Meaning: SEX APPEAL

Sex appeal isn't about perfection, size, or looks—it's about the feelings you exude. What are you telling the world with your vibes? Experiment with exuding sexuality, and watch what happens!

Her History

With her enduring legacy, Marilyn Monroe is still a queen of the silver screen. Born Norma Jean Mortenson, this sweet girl had a rocky start to life, being shuffled around foster homes and orphanages. By the age of five, she dreamt of acting, realizing that it lifted her out of the heaviness of her daily life. At 16, when faced with having to go to a different orphanage, she opted to marry her 21-year-old boyfriend and get out of the foster care system. Two years later, her husband was in the South Pacific with the Marines, and she was working at a local munitions factory. One day, on a routine photography assignment, the Army came to film the women at work. She was a natural in front of the camera. That was the day her star power was discovered. She quickly dyed her hair blond, quit working at the factory, divorced her husband, and took on as many modeling jobs as she could—all to focus entirely on her career. It was then that she picked her perfect screen name: Marilyn Monroe.

At first, Marilyn was thought of as too shy and soft-spoken to become a real actress by directors and acting teachers, but she knew what she was capable of. Determined to be taken seriously, she spent years learning from the best schools and teachers in Hollywood. She took small parts at first, but in the early 1950s began to catch some breakthrough roles. Once the public met Marilyn, she became an overnight sensation. Despite her concerns about her ability to act, her hard work and natural magnetism paid off, as she rose to enormous fame and adoration.

Marilyn's beauty, brilliance, and sunny outward appearance masked her struggles with fame and the pressure of being constantly in the spotlight. Serious anxiety and stress led Marilyn to use pharmaceuticals to cope, and in 1962, at the age of 36, Marilyn ended her life through an overdose of her medications. The world has grieved her loss ever since but keeps her alive as the eternal queen of old Hollywood glamour and as the ultimate American beauty. Marilyn is still the subject of countless pieces of art, books, songs, and movies. Though her life was short, her impact is lasting.

Bless this woman for the playfulness, femininity, and charm that she gifted to the world.

Martha Stewart
b. 1941

"Life is too complicated not to be orderly."

Meaning: GET IT TOGETHER

Get. It. Together. Both your outer material world and your inner emotional and energetic world need tending to. The more organized you make your outer world, the more space you'll have to clear out old experiences and emotions that are no longer serving you. The more you deal with inner tumult, the easier it will be to keep your outer world clean and healthy. Take the time to be a little domestic when it comes to your care. Your space is an extension of you; what is it telling you?

Also, know that perfection is overrated. Martha Stewart may appear to be perfectly pressed and able to juggle it all, but that's just a persona. It's important to get messy sometimes, let your hair down, and make mistakes—it's the only way you'll learn.

Alternate Meaning: DOMESTICITY

It's time to get domestic. At times, the rise of independence, modernism, and the busyness of the world devalues the sacredness of home. We forget the sanctity of caring for others, baking, cooking, cleaning, and the importance of other domestic roles and tasks. There is pleasure to be had in these skills and hobbies. Explore which domestic activities you enjoy—don't write them off as frivolous or unworthy of your time.

Her History

This Jersey City-born girl was one of six children in a middle-class Polish family. Martha's mother was a homemaker who taught her how to sew and cook, while her father taught her how to garden.

Her grandmother taught her how to preserve foods and make jams. All of the children were expected to do chores and help with the care of their home. These early daily routines and lessons would form the future of Martha's success and expertise.

Martha has worked her entire life. She babysat and organized children's parties in her teen years and then worked as a model to support herself through college, where she earned two degrees: one in history and another in architectural history. After college, she married and began stock trading on the New York Stock Exchange. She excelled at trading, but it was when she began to refurbish her and her husband's 1800s farmhouse in Connecticut that her natural skill for design and decoration became instantly apparent. Shortly after, she started a catering company that attracted the attention of publishing CEOs who requested that she write a cookbook. The rest is homemaking dynasty history. A tenacious businesswoman and prolific writer, she produced eight books between 1984 and 1989 alone.

By the early 1990s, book deals became magazine deals, magazine deals become television show deals, and the Martha Stewart brand has been growing ever since. Martha revolutionized and popularized American homemaking. Her prowess in the home sphere is equally matched by her business savvy. She has created success wherever she sets her sights. She's mastered the arts of publishing, book writing, e-commerce, broadcasting, television, design, and merchandising.

Nothing can keep Martha down. Even after being convicted for insider trading in 2004, she made a complete comeback, regaining full control of her companies. The world had assumed that would have been the end of Martha, but with her unstoppable determination, she climbed back on top and has created new project after new project and more success than ever. A tycoon in the lifestyle space, Martha Stewart has earned her place as a household name.

Thanks to this woman for her hustle, her love of the home, and the never-ending wellspring of ways in which she has impacted American life.

Maya Angelou
1928-2014

"Nothing can dim the light that shines within."

Meaning: FREEDOM

Let Maya Angelou inspire you to set yourself free and shine who you truly are into your world. You are a creative creature, made by a creative universe, and a creation is ready to move through you. It needs no reason, no logic, nor purpose. The beauty, feelings, words, and songs within you are meant to be in this world and not sit inside your imagination. Take pleasure in your expression and the way you live. Radiate it. Do it for you.

True freedom comes from within. Free yourself through your unedited expression of who you are. Do what you do because it feels good and because it makes you happy—those are the only reasons you need to do anything.

Alternate Meaning: PROCESS

Remember to respect the process. Be present with your journey. You are in one phase of your grand and varied life. Enjoy it as it is right now, and know that one day it will change and carry you to new horizons.

Her History

This bright soul was born in St. Louis, Missouri, but became a global citizen in her life. Her childhood was marked with darkness after she was raped at the age of eight. For the next five years, she didn't speak a word. Out of this time came her love of writing and observation. Eventually, she spoke again, and by the age of 16, she was the first Black female cable car operator in San Francisco. That same year, she also became pregnant. She decided to raise her son alone, rather than marry a man she didn't love simply to meet society's expectations.

With a deep love of dance, she began to study singing, dance, and poetry. In 1945, she landed a role with the international *Porgy and Bess* show, performing in 22 countries in one year. That show inspired her first album, then led her to perform off-Broadway and in her first film. She joined the Harlem Writers Guild and was introduced to many famous Black artists, as well as Martin Luther King Jr. In those years, she pressed against the barriers of what a Black woman was allowed to be, resisting the suppression that could have made her less powerful than she was. Over the next decade, she lived around the globe as a newspaper editor, civil rights activist, and performer, then ended up back in New York City, where a friend challenged her to write an autobiography.

This autobiography, *I Know Why the Caged Bird Sings,* chronicled her life from ages three to 16, capturing her transition from a girl to a woman, the trauma and healing of her rape, her struggle against racist repression, motherhood, and the challenges of living in a world ruled by men. It inspired liberation and living life to its fullest, even in the face of adversity and oppression. She was one of the first women to speak of the innermost details of her life and the realities of Black life. This book stayed on the *New York Times* bestseller list for two years and lifted her to enormous fame.

Maya had a prolific career. She composed songs for musicians and movie scores, acted, directed, produced plays, and wrote short stories, poetry, six more autobiographies, scripts, and documentaries. She became a college professor and lecturer and was awarded over 30 honorary degrees from universities around the globe.

Through her bare and truthful writing, Maya Angelou set herself and others free. Her creations remain as beacons of honesty, possibility, and the resilience of the human spirit.

Thanks to this woman for giving herself so fully to life and for boldly empowering others to do the same.

Michelle Obama
b. 1964

> "When someone is cruel or acts like a bully, you don't stoop to their level. No, our motto is: when they go low, we go high."

Meaning: INTEGRITY

No one benefits when we stoop low. Hold a high bar for how you relate to the world. Never let the way that other people act be an excuse to retaliate or act contrary to your own integrity. Watch for people trying to get a rise out of you — they are trying to bring you down to make themselves feel better. Don't take the bait.

Michelle is a true lady, but being a lady isn't about being repressed and stuffy — it's about acting with honor and kindness. Model these qualities. This doesn't mean that you don't speak up for yourself and your rights — you just do it in a way that doesn't cut others down. Practice embodying the stance of a lady. Stand upright with your head held high. Do this every day before you engage with the world. It will build your confidence and help you rise above the noise of anything that could bring you down.

Alternate Meaning: HEALTH

Your body needs you to move it daily, to eat fresh foods, and to change your routines to support lifelong vibrancy and well-being. It's not a phase or a passing trend — we all need preventative care and movement in our lives.

Her History

A bold and brilliant icon, Michelle Obama was born to hold her head high. Southside Chicago born and raised, she was a natural achiever, determined to do well for herself. By sixth grade, she was placed in a school for gifted children, then attended Chicago's first magnet high school. She took advanced placement classes, became the student council treasurer, earned a place in the National Honor Society, and graduated at the top of her class. Her hard work and perseverance earned her entry first to Princeton and then Harvard Law School.

While in college, she became acutely aware of the opportunity disparities among races, which inspired her to build a career around social justice. In 1989, while working at her first law firm, Michelle was charged with mentoring a new associate by the name of Barack Obama. Little did she know that this would be her future husband and the 44th president of the United States. On that day, her fate was sealed to become the first Black first lady of the United States.

Michelle is an articulate and inspirational human who has bloomed wherever she has been planted. She has excelled as a lawyer, a wife, a mother, a fundraiser, an executive director, a campaigner, and a board member, and she became one of the fiercest first ladies the United States has ever seen.

Known for her elegance, intelligence, and style, Michelle applied her passion to a wide variety of causes during the eight years she served as first lady. She championed causes like education, equal opportunity for girls, health and fitness, and veteran support. On January 20, 2017, Michelle left the White House at the end of President Obama's two terms. As a first lady, she is remembered as a woman eternally on a mission. She has gone on to write a bestselling memoir—traveling the world speaking to and inspiring millions. In 2020, she became the centerpiece of a biographical documentary, and in the same year, her production company won an Oscar for another documentary. Michelle can be counted on to be out in the world, every day, using her power for the greatest good.

Big thanks to this powerful and wise woman who inspires us to be the best version of ourselves.

Nina Simone
1933-2003

"I am a rebel—with a cause."

Meaning: REBEL

What really matters to you? Are you idly standing by while things, people, places, and causes you care about are struggling? Nina Simone faced and spoke out against injustices for her entire life. She made it hard for people to ignore the things that she cared for deeply. She actively rebelled against oppressive authority, racism, and outdated social norms. She used her voice, career, and body to advocate for the well-being of others and the world at large.

Living with your head in the sand moves you away from your power. You may have to face discomfort standing up for what you believe in, but it's a million times better than a life half lived. When you speak up, others may judge you, friends may feel uneasy, and you may receive backlash. Still, stay true to yourself. You are more powerful than you think. Through your standing up for your beliefs, you will embolden others to do the same.

Alternate Meaning: TAKE UP SPACE

Nina Simone never made herself small to make others feel more comfortable. Stop shrinking. Speak your needs. Practice stretching your body to its full size and span. Use the fullness of your voice to fill a room. Take up space. You are meant to be here.

Her History

This force of nature was born with a fiery spirit. Nina was one of eight children, raised by soulful parents in rural North Carolina. When playing the piano at three years old, her natural talent was revealed. At her first recital, Nina's parents were forced to sit at the back of the hall and give up their seats for white people. She refused to play until they were sat in the front row. This was her first experience with racism and the first, but not last, time she would take a stand for her beliefs.

Nina's piano teacher and local community raised funds for her schooling. She attended an all-girls high school and went on to study at Juilliard in New York City. After being denied entry to the Curtis Institute of Music, she took a job playing the piano at a bar in Atlantic City, New Jersey. The owner told her she'd have to sing to accompany her piano playing, and that was the birth of Nina Simone: singer, performer, rebel, and songwriter.

Nina fused blues, soul, gospel, and classical music into her own magical style. In 1958, her version of "I Loves You Porgy" landed on the Top 20 Billboard hits in the US. She then released her first successful record, *Little Girl Blue*. In the 1960s, she released more records and began to reflect the outer world in her music. She cemented herself as a fierce Civil Rights activist when she released the song "Mississippi Goddam," which she performed in response to the killing of Medgar Evers and the 1963 bombing of the 16th Street Baptist Church in Birmingham, Alabama. There was no silencing Nina Simone. She addressed racial inequalities and violence more than any other entertainer of her day. She was a devoted supporter of Malcolm X and performed at many of the most prominent Civil Rights protests of her era, including the Selma-to-Montgomery marches with Martin Luther King Jr.

Though at times it hurt her career, Nina believed that it was her duty as an artist to express what was happening in the world around her. She spent her entire life rebelling against oppression. She rebelled against Eurocentric beauty standards and encouraged Black women to find their own definition of beauty that was free from societal norms. In the '70s, she spoke out against the Vietnam War and eventually moved away from the US when she felt unsupported as a revolutionary. Throughout her entire life, she never stopped using her voice, she never stopped creating soulful and rare music, and she always took a stand for what she believed in.

Blessings to this brilliant woman, this rebellious and artistic soul, for all the courage and creativity she shared with the world in her lifetime.

Oprah Winfrey
b. 1954

> "As far back as I can recall, my prayer has been the same: Use me, God. Show me how to take who I am, who I want to be, and what I can do, and use it for a purpose greater than myself."

Meaning: DIVINE CHANNEL

It's time to get tapped in. Tap into the force in the Universe that bestows gifts upon you and brings the lessons that you need to evolve in this lifetime. Connect to and trust in a Higher Power. It doesn't matter what you call that Higher Power. It's here waiting to support you in your endeavors. Open to its signs. Hear its call, and radiate its inspiration to the world. You are here to uplift humanity, and that Higher Power is here to help you.

You are never alone. Speak to your Higher Power. Ask it for help, and thank it for every little thing it gives you. The more gratitude you have, the more it will give to you. It wants to give to you because it loves you and knows that the more you are given, the more you will share. You are a divine channel in this lifetime—it's time to heed the call.

Alternate Meaning: PRAY

When did you last pray? Never underestimate the power of asking for what you need. How can the world deliver if it can't hear you? How will it know where to deliver your blessings? It's time to make prayer a daily ritual.

Her History

This all-powerful soul came to bring light and understanding to this world. Oprah had humble beginnings in Kosciusko, Mississippi, where her family was so poor that she often wore potato sacks because they couldn't afford to clothe her. Her young years were fraught with difficulties. She endured sexual abuse, extreme poverty, and being bounced back and forth between living with her mother and father in Wisconsin and Tennessee.

By her mid-teens, she settled in Tennessee, where her father encouraged her to apply herself fully at school. Despite her early years of strife, she rose to the occasion, becoming an honors student, joining the speech team, and winning an oratory contest, which earned her a scholarship to Tennessee State University. Her natural prowess with speech caught the attention of a local news station, and that was the beginning of Oprah's long, evocative, and inspiring career.

Oprah jumped from station to station, from Nashville to Boston and finally to Chicago, where she was charged with hosting the city's lowest-rated talk show. Within months, the show was revived and became the highest-rated talk show in the city. The show was lengthened to an hour and renamed *The Oprah Winfrey Show*, which went on to air 4,561 episodes over 25 seasons and became one of the most impactful television shows of all time.

Oprah easily became the queen of the talk shows and transformed the terrain of television. She ushered in a wave of growth, self-help, and love into the nation in the late '80s. She did this through the topics she chose for her show, and she hasn't stopped inspiring since. Through her hard work and determination, she became the wealthiest Black American of the 20th century and America's first Black multibillionaire.

Often ranked as the most influential woman in the world—and certainly a powerhouse of talents—Oprah has held the positions of talk show host, chairwoman, CEO, chief creative officer, author, producer, award-winning actor, media executive, philanthropist, and more. She has been awarded the Presidential Medal of Freedom, granted honorary degrees from Harvard and Duke, received numerous accolades throughout her career, and still isn't even close to finished with creating her personal and powerful imprint on this world.

So many thanks to Oprah for helping us to become the best versions of ourselves and for inspiring us with her never-ending faithfulness, service, and care for this world.

Patsy Mink
1927–2002

> "It's easy enough to vote right and consistently be with the majority. But it is often more important to be ahead of the majority, and this means being willing to cut the first furrow in the ground and stand alone for a while if necessary."

Meaning: INDEPENDENCE

Your independence and free thinking are the keys to your success. We have all given too much power away to the noise, information sources, and opinions of others. Dig into details before you believe something. Prioritize your autonomy. Stand on your own two feet. Create financial independence. Take time to check in with yourself on what really matters to you—today, this week, this month, and in this lifetime. You can be fully independent and easily have relationships with others when you take the time to be true to yourself first.

Alternate Meaning: EDUCATION

Education equals opportunity. That's why Patsy Mink worked so hard to transform school funding. Learn something new. Add a new tool to your toolbox. Open your opportunities through building your education.

Her History

Patsy Mink (née Takemoto), the granddaughter of Japanese immigrants, was born in Hawaii, where she experienced inequities among white, Native, and Japanese residents. She saw her father, the first Japanese American to graduate from the University of Hawaii with a degree in civil engineering, lose promotions that went to his white peers. Her family experienced discrimination after the bombing of Pearl Harbor for being Japanese, and as life went on, she continued to confront racial and gender discrimination.

A sharp student, Patsy graduated valedictorian of her high school. She then attended the University of Hawaii before she attended mainland colleges. In Nebraska, she was angered to find students racially segregated in the dorms (and more), so she organized a coalition of alumni, parents, students, businesses, and teachers that within one year ended the segregation.

Patsy earned degrees in biology and zoology and dreamt of going to medical school but wasn't admitted to any because she was a woman. Frustrated, she pivoted to studying law at the University of Chicago as one of only two women in her class. It was there that she met her husband. Because she was a woman, Asian American, and interracially married, law firms would not hire her while she tried to secure her first job.

Patsy and her family moved back to Hawaii. She passed the bar exam, becoming the first Japanese American woman licensed to practice law there. Still, no one hired her, so she formed her own practice. At the age of 29, Patsy ran for Hawaii's House of Representatives (without the support of the local Democratic party because she was a woman). She won and became quickly known for her independence and fight for equality and education. A powerful Civil Rights ally, she won a seat in the US House of Representatives in 1965—becoming the first woman of color elected to the House. She held that position for six terms, from 1965 to 1977.

Patsy was the first woman of color to deliver a State of the Union address. She spoke out against the Vietnam War and the abysmal state of civil rights in the US. She coauthored and fought for the hugely impactful passage of Title IX, which finally prohibited sex-based discrimination in schools. She was the assistant secretary for oceans and environmental affairs, advocating for animal protection and against deep-sea mining. In 1990, she returned to Congress for an additional six terms. At the age of 74, Patsy passed away, just one week after she won her 2002 primary. She was so loved that Hawaiians posthumously reelected her to her congressional seat.

Let us honor Patsy for her impact on the lives of women around the world and her dedication to equality, education, and opportunities for all.

Queen Elizabeth II
1926-2022

"It has been women who have breathed gentleness and care into the hard progress of mankind."

Meaning: FEMININITY

It's time to help balance our masculine world with your feminine traits. All of us have masculine and feminine characteristics, and they need each other to thrive. Our world has historically been dominated by the ideals of masculine progress, but it's time for greater balance. The world is calling to the feminine for help. Where can you infuse feminine gentleness and care? Does your work or home need more presence, tenderness, and inclusion?

Do you need to breathe gentleness into yourself, your body, and your own personal life? Are you trying to grow without giving yourself time to integrate your lessons, loves, heartbreaks, and successes? Are you making enough time to celebrate the progress that you do achieve? How balanced are your feminine qualities like patience, intuition, flexibility, and nurturing? Taking the time to develop these traits will benefit you and the world around you greatly.

Alternate Meaning: DURATION

Life is long. Make sure you know how to take care of yourself. Try not to take everything too seriously. You need levity to sustain your energy for the tasks at hand and to enjoy the rich life ahead of you!

Her History

This literal queen is one for the history books. Elizabeth, who took to the throne of Britain at the age of 25, is the matriarch supreme. She was the longest-serving female monarch in history. One of the most visible figures of the 20th and 21st centuries, she inspired and guided not only Great Britain but the entire globe in her 96 years of life.

Elizabeth's fate was sealed when her uncle abdicated the throne, making her father the new king of the United Kingdom. From an early age, she had a great sense of duty and sensibility, which she infused into every decision of her reign. In her late childhood and teenage years, Elizabeth turned toward public service, being slowly prepared for the faraway day when she would take the throne. But her father, King George VI, died unexpectedly early, crowning Elizabeth to queendom decades before anyone expected.

A pillar of consistency, Queen Elizabeth nobly navigated decades of massive change. She led the UK in its transition from a global empire to a more consolidated state and helped it move through the dramatic social and religious changes that occurred across the world during the '50s, '60s, and '70s. Elizabeth did this all while being steadfast in her loyalty to the British people.

Throughout her reign, but particularly in the '90s, she began to open up the royal family and Buckingham Palace to the public, demystifying and evolving royal life by bringing the monarchy and people closer together.

The years passed, public perception ebbed and flowed, global events shook and destabilized the world around her, but Elizabeth remained steady. She served as a role model for her entire life and showed the world how much power and capability women have. She proved that femininity is a vital trait in our modern and masculine world. Elizabeth, like many women, was deeply underestimated but surpassed every expectation that was placed on her. A faithful and devoted public servant every day of her life, she carried the UK and the monarchy into the modern world with grace and dignity.

Bless this woman and the world she so steadily carried—both in her heart and on her shoulders.

Rachel Carson
1907-1964

> "The more clearly we can focus our attention on the wonders and realities of the universe about us, the less taste we will have for destruction."

Meaning: EARTH GUARDIAN

Mother Earth is calling you to her. Spend time in her rivers, lakes, and oceans. Nourish your senses with her lush and vibrant life. She feels that you are out of balance, and so is she. Connect with her so that she can help heal you. She needs you to help heal her in return. Make time to place your bare feet on the ground, breathe deeply, and take in your surroundings. Listen to the sounds. Take in the colors and smells. This will help bring balance to your life and soothe your body's ailments.

The earth needs you to step up. This can be as small as picking up one piece of trash a day or as great as starting a business or nonprofit that supports environmental causes. Buy goods that are made in harmony with the environment and the other nonhuman animals that live here. Remember, this entire earth is your home; you are responsible for caring for it.

Alternate Meaning: TECHNOLOGY

Get off of that computer, that phone, or any other device. You need a tech break. Make time for when your phone isn't with you. Trade your electronic time for nature or for human connection. Use it; don't let it use you.

Her History

Born deeply connected to the earth, Rachel spent her childhood roaming her family's 65-acre farm in Pennsylvania, often preferring the company of animals to that of humans. A natural writer, she published her first story at age 10. She graduated at the top of her class, then went on to earn a bachelor's in biology at Pennsylvania College for Women.

Focused on environmental learning, she went to Johns Hopkins for her master's in science. In 1934, en route to getting her doctorate, the Great Depression struck, and Rachel moved home to support her family.

Destiny kept her on track when a temp job writing radio copy for a weekly series called *Romance Under the Sea* opened at the US Bureau of Fisheries. Many writers had tried and failed to generate public excitement with the series, but Rachel's passion for biology and imaginative writing made all the difference. At the end of the contract, she was hired full-time, only the second woman to fill a permanent position at the bureau.

She spent her days in the field collecting and assessing data, then writing brochures and other literature. Soon came book writing, and in 1941, she published *Under the Sea Wind*, the first in a trilogy of books that explored sea life in depth. Her next book, *The Sea Around Us*, examined the formation of the earth, moon, and seas, for which she won a US National Book Award and became the public voice for support of the sciences. She completed the trilogy with *The Edge of the Sea*.

Next, she began to examine the increasingly popular use of pesticides, which she discovered were biocides—substances capable of killing all life—not just pests. In 1962, after years of research, she published *Silent Spring*, which placed a national spotlight on environmental issues. She was met with heavy criticism from chemical companies, but *Silent Spring* led to US policy reform and a ban on the toxic chemical DDT. *Silent Spring* created a grassroots movement, which birthed the US Environmental Protection Agency (EPA), making Rachel the mother of US environmentalism.

Two years after *Silent Spring* was published, Rachel Carson passed away, but her mission lives on in the movements she spurred through her love of the earth. For her great work, she was awarded the Presidential Medal of Freedom in 1980.

Thanks to this woman for her tireless work to protect the earth and all of its creatures.

Ruth Bader Ginsburg
1933-2020

"Fight for the things that you care about, but do it in a way that will lead others to join you."

Meaning: TAKE THE LEAD

The Notorious RBG could teach you a thing or two about leadership. Ask yourself: "Am I creating inclusion or separation with my opinions and actions?" Step back from the current situation at hand. Can you speak and lead in a way that doesn't judge or make assumptions about others? How well do you understand the experience of others? Do you have enough information?

Real leaders take responsibility for the part they play in any situation. They seek information and understanding before making decisions about anyone or anything. They work hard to care for their team, crew, and families, and they always have the best interests of all in mind. Let RBG inspire you (today!) to release yourself from judgment. See beyond appearances, genders, and skin colors. Find common ground with those around you, both near and far.

Alternate Meaning: DISCRIMINATION

Don't discriminate against anyone for any reason. If you are discriminating, it's due to your own small-mindedness or fears that keep you from finding value in others. We all have value, and we all deserve kindness.

Her History

This brilliant Brooklyn-born game changer came into this life with strength to share. Ruth's mother was also brilliant but unable to attend college because her family couldn't afford it. Instead, Ruth's mother took an active role in Ruth's education to ensure her daughter's success. Ruth excelled academically and got into Cornell University after high school. She graduated at the top of her class with a degree in government. Upon graduating, she married her college sweetheart and started her first job, but she was quickly demoted when she became pregnant.

Within a year of giving birth, Ruth enrolled at Harvard Law School as one of nine women in a class of 500. She and her female classmates had an uphill battle, consistently being criticized for taking the place of male students. When her young family moved to New York, she transferred to Columbia University and graduated first in her class. Despite her brilliance, she faced gender discrimination professionally, but one of her college professors intervened and encouraged a judge to hire her. She clerked for two years before transitioning into academia at Rutgers Law School. This was a prestigious position, but she was still paid much less than her male counterparts. All of her experiences gave her a keen eye for inequality and a desire to level the playing field for all genders, ages, nationalities, and races.

In the '70s, Ruth founded the *Women's Rights Law Reporter* and cofounded the Women's Rights Project of the American Civil Liberties Union (ACLU). In its first year, the Women's Rights Project took on over 300 gender discrimination suits, and by 1976, Ruth had won five Supreme Court cases. She became known for strategically creating change rather than pushing for too much at once so that lasting transformations in equality could take place.

In 1980, President Jimmy Carter nominated Ruth to the US Court of Appeals, where she served until 1993, when President Bill Clinton elevated her to the US Supreme Court. Ruth was the second woman and first Jewish Supreme Court judge. Despite her liberal and evolving views, she was a unifying force across many perspectives and cases. She influenced the most important cases of the 20th century, and in the 21st century, she became a vision of feminism and passion embodied by her refusal to step down from the Supreme Court until the day she died.

So many thanks to this loyal and royal public servant for her lifelong work of steadily bringing equality to all.

Sandra Day O'Connor
b. 1930

> "We don't accomplish anything in the world alone—whatever happens is the result of the whole tapestry of one's life and all the weavings of individual threads from one to another."

Meaning: COME TOGETHER

It's time to pool together your resources, friends, family, and coworkers and bring them together for a common cause. The world needs more caring community. You have the ability to unite people and create a positive impact. Find a cause near and dear to your heart, and ask people to support both you and this thing you cherish. We all gain so much when we give and work together.

It's also time to give thanks to everyone and everything that has gotten you to where you are, even the challenges, for they, too, create the unique landscape of your individual, human experience. Remember, we humans are designed to be together, to collaborate, and to support each other. Don't go it alone.

Alternate Meaning: GLASS CEILING

Break through the glass ceiling. The outdated structures, roles, and jobs in this world are calling out to you to come and redefine them. Pioneer on!

Her History

This all-powerful soul came to bring light and understanding to this world. Sandra, an honorable and brilliant woman, began her life hunting and farming on her parents' Arizona cattle ranch. She was a natural on the ranch but even more of a natural in academics. Her parents placed a high value on learning and sent her to live with her grandmother in Texas during the school year. She excelled, and at only 16 years old, she was accepted into Stanford University. She earned her economics degree (in three years, instead of the usual four) and then attended Stanford's prestigious law school in an era when most law schools didn't even allow women to apply.

Despite the fact that she graduated in the top 10 percent of her class, when she tried to find work, she was confronted with an industry entirely unwelcoming to women. Sandra was repeatedly rejected from applying or interviewing for open law positions all over the country simply because she was a woman. In order to secure her first job, she agreed to work for free and share her desk with the secretary. She was committed to her career despite the sacrifices she had to make and the uphill battle she had to climb.

When her husband was drafted in World War II, she moved overseas with him and became a civilian attorney for the Army Corps. When they returned to the States three years later, Sandra took five years off to raise her three sons, but as soon as she could, she jumped back into law and was off to the races. She established her own private practice, and only eight years later, she was serving as the assistant attorney general of Arizona.

In 1969, she was appointed to a vacant Arizona Senate seat and then served two full terms as an elected official. By 1973, she was the first female Senate majority leader, and from 1975 to 1979, she served on the Arizona Court of Appeals. She became known nationally for her keen skills of negotiation and moderate opinions, which got the attention of President Ronald Reagan. In 1981, President Reagan appointed her as the first female Supreme Court justice in the US. Sandra Day O'Connor served on the Supreme Court as one of the most powerful women in the world for 25 years before her retirement.

Blessings to this intelligent and determined woman for all her years of service and for opening doors for so many women who came after her.

Serena & Venus Williams
b. 1981 & 1980

> "The successes of every woman should be inspiration to another. We should raise each other up." — Serena

> "The message I like to convey to women and girls across the globe is that there is no glass ceiling." — Venus

Meaning: SISTERHOOD

You are supported by a vast sisterhood of women reaching far and wide through space and time. The sisterhood among women is sacred. It's here to uplift you and build your confidence. Whether or not you have sisters or a visible community of women in your life, the power and love of the sisterhood supports you. When feeling doubt, uncertainty, or loneliness, call on the invisible thread of power that has been connecting women since the dawn of time. Ask it to bring powerful women into your life who will propel your growth and success.

Don't forget to support the success of other women. Applaud them. Compliment them. Ask if there are ways you can support their dreams. There is enough abundance, beauty, wealth, and power for us all. It's not a competition. Focus on being the best version of yourself, for yourself. Don't let your success come at the detriment of other sisters.

Alternate Meaning: WORK IT OUT

Move. Get vigorous exercise—your body needs it. Build your muscles and endurance. Doing this is going to stabilize your body, spirit, emotions, and mind while also building your confidence.

Their History

These sisters were raised in Compton, California, and as soon as they were born, they were set on their powerhouse paths. By the time they could walk, they were playing tennis. Their father was determined that his daughters would have every opportunity in life and saw tennis as the way to make that happen. The girls were homeschooled from their elementary through high school years to create more practice time. Their father learned everything he could about the game and taught them both with exuberance. The girls were inherently athletic and took to sports easily. In the '90s, the family moved to Florida so the girls could receive the best tennis training available at one of the top tennis schools in the country. For the next four years, they trained six hours a day, six days a week. All the practice and hard work paid off.

These women were born to compete and win. By their teens, they went professional and received $12 million in sponsorships. Each sister has traveled the world, dominating and shaking up the game of tennis. They have won every possible tennis championship, broken every record, earned Olympic gold medals, and have inspired millions of women and girls—particularly Black girls—to pursue their interests with vigor.

Venus and Serena uplift and inspire each other to be the best versions of themselves. They are the best female tennis players of all time and icons of physical prowess. Over the years, they have become equally powerful off the court as both fashion stars and savvy businesswomen. Determined to uplift others, they dedicate time and resources to helping low-income children have greater access to sports lessons and opportunities. They are minority owners of the Miami Dolphins and are the first Black women to own an NFL team.

The Williams sisters have been demolishing tennis tournaments for two decades and show no signs of dwindling skill or competitive edge. They are both dynamic and mighty role models who have created a legacy of inspiration.

Many thanks to these triumphant sisters and their profound and power-filled legacy.

Sylvia Rivera
1951–2002

"We have to be visible. We should not be ashamed of who we are."

Meaning: VISIBILITY

It is time to let yourself be seen for exactly who you are. It is also time for you to see yourself for exactly who you are. We often learn to hide the most unique or different parts of ourselves, but that can leave us feeling less than whole. Gathering up all your different parts is an act of healing for you and an act of inspiration for others.

Maybe in the past you weren't given the support you needed when expressing your truest self, leaving you feeling ashamed or guarded. Now you can learn to give yourself the love and support you need to be fully you. You deserve to be yourself, and the world is ready to see you. It may take vulnerability and courage, but it's time.

Alternate Meaning: COMMUNITY

Surround yourself with like-minded community and kindred souls. See and feel this understanding community coming your way, surrounding you with love and nourishment.

Her History

Sylvia was born in the Bronx to a Puerto Rican father and a Venezuelan mother. She was assigned male at birth. Her childhood was filled with heartache—her father disappeared after she was born, and her mother committed suicide after enduring an abusive marriage. For some years, she was raised by her grandmother, but the more she began to express herself as a girl, the more her grandmother disapproved of and abused her. She was harassed at school for acting like a girl. At the age of 11, she ran away from home. She lived on the streets, working as a child prostitute near Times Square, in an area frequented by drag queens. It was ultimately that community that took her in and helped her become "Sylvia." She first identified as a drag queen and later as a trans woman.

In 1963, Sylvia met Marsha P. Johnson, a Black drag queen and activist, who shaped Sylvia's life. Together, they fought for the inclusion of trans people and people of color into the larger gay-rights movement. After the Stonewall riots, a series of protests in Greenwich Village that were pivotal to the elevation of the gay-rights movement, Sylvia continued the momentum. She founded Street Transvestite Action Revolutionaries (STAR) with Marsha; they advocated for homeless gay, trans, and gender-fluid youths.

As a trans woman, Latina, person of color, prior sex worker, and someone who dealt with on-and-off drug abuse and homelessness, Sylvia found herself taking a stand for not only gay rights but racial, economic, and criminal justice issues. She became known as one of the most radical activists of the '60s and '70s but ultimately moved to upstate New York in the '80s to take a break after feeling minimized and written out of the larger gay-rights movement. After the death of her good friend and ally Marsha P. Johnson, Sylvia returned to NYC to pick up the fight for the inclusion of transgender people, especially youths. She worked for this cause until she passed away from liver cancer in 2002. Sylvia lives on through the work of the Sylvia Rivera Law Project, which works to guarantee the freedom and safety of self-determination of gender for all—regardless of race or income.

In 2005, an intersection was named after her in Greenwich Village. In 2015, she was the first transgender person to be added to the Smithsonian Museum's National Portrait Gallery, and a statue is being erected in New York to honor Sylvia and Marsha for their pioneering activism.

Thanks to Sylvia for her commitment to freedom of expression for every kind of human being.

Toni Morrison
1931-2019

> "Make up a story.... For our sake and yours, forget your name in the street; tell us what the world has been to you in the dark places and the light."

Meaning: WRITE

Write, write, then write some more. Write your heart out. You have words, stories, needs, emotions, and experiences filling up your body, and they need to get out. Write until your hands ache from the grasp of your pen. Explore the complexity of your human experience by writing about your feelings and deepest desires. Write the things you would never dare say. Free yourself from any judgment and shame, and let the words and feelings flow.

Let your writing be an outlet for the hard times and a celebratory record of the good ones. Write before you go to bed to appreciate the beauty of your days. Write a loving letter to someone who could benefit from a thoughtful word. Use your imagination to transform the most mundane moments into those filled with treasure and delight. Know yourself through your writing—ask your body, heart, mind, and soul how they're doing, and see what they need. One day, share your writing with others. That, too, will nourish you.

Alternate Meaning: BOOKS

Surround yourself with books. Read tenaciously. Take in stories—the more vivid and imaginative the better. Feed your senses with colorful tales and otherworldly scenes. Let the written word infiltrate every corner of your life.

Her History

This heartful woman was born and raised in Lorain, Ohio. Despite the challenges her family faced—racism, poverty, and living through the Great Depression—her parents modeled grace in the face of adversity.

They also infused Black pride and heritage into their children through traditional songs, myths, and folk tales. Toni's early family life greatly informed her creativity. A top student, Toni attended Howard University, one of the United States' top historically Black universities. She then earned her master's at Cornell University, which opened the door for her to teach college literature.

In her mid-20s, she married and had two sons, but by the age of 33, Toni was divorced and moved to New York City for an editing job. Within two years, she became the first Black female senior editor at Random House Publishing, where she had a massive impact on introducing African American literature into the mainstream. Toni helped create a national and public voice for the lives and struggles of Black Americans in the US.

In the late '60s, Toni began to pen her first novel. She had to wake at 4 a.m. daily to write before her children woke. In 1970, *The Bluest Eye* was published to critical praise for her poetic and folklore-infused style of writing. Toni's third novel, *Song of Solomon*, won a National Book Critics Circle Award and an American Academy of Arts and Letters Award.

By the late '70s, Toni was a well-known author, particularly for the way she honored Black culture and struggles. In 1987, she published *Beloved* to international acclaim and received a Pulitzer Prize in Fiction. In 1993, she was honored as the first Black woman to receive the Nobel Prize in Literature for her poeticism and her remarkable contribution to modern literature.

Toni Morrison went on to receive the highest honors across the United States, including the Presidential Medal of Freedom for her contributions to literature, Black American life, and history. Widely considered the greatest American novelist, Toni has inspired generations of writers through her beautiful and painful storytelling and her imaginative style of prose.

Bless this woman and the imaginative, deep, and healing impact she had on the lives of so many.

Wilma Mankiller
1945-2010

> "The most fulfilled people are the ones who get up every morning and stand for something larger than themselves."

Meaning: LEND A HAND

Our capitalist society may consistently tell us that we need more—more stuff, more money, more achievements, and the list goes on. It is not material wealth and things that are going to bring you the greatest happiness. It's caring for others and working for something greater than yourself. The fulfillment you crave will come from the care you give. This might be through acts of kindness, gifting your time and energy to causes in your community, or a new career that gives back to people and places. Remember, study after study has proven that the act of giving is what leads to deep and lasting happiness.

Alternate Meaning: INTERCONNECTEDNESS

Everything we do touches others, our surroundings, and our environment. Feel into the ways we are all connected, and reflect on what impact you want to have on our world. Align your desired impact with your actions.

Her History

Wilma Mankiller was born in Tahlequah, Oklahoma—the capital of the Cherokee Nation. Her unique last name came from her father's lineage, which refers to a traditional Cherokee military rank. Her family, with 11 children, lived in a small house with no electricity or plumbing. She didn't realize that they lived in poverty. She loved this time—living off the land, hunting, and being immersed in her Cherokee heritage.

Financially struggling, they moved to San Francisco as a part of the Indian Relocation Act, a law that moved Native families off reservations to assimilate them into the general population. Wilma was only 11, and she found life in the city away from her tribe very difficult.

At times, Wilma struggled academically, but she still graduated high school. By 19, she was a married mother. After the birth of her second daughter, she went to junior college and became inspired by Native American and civil rights groups. She supported the occupation of Alcatraz, helped northern California tribes reclaim tribal lands, and drafted legislation to protect Native children from being taken from their families. In the late '70s, Wilma went home to Oklahoma. She finished college while creating the Community Development Department of the Cherokee Nation, where she raised millions of dollars and managed beneficial community projects. So impressed, the Chief asked Wilma to be his running mate in the next election. He won, making her the first female deputy chief of the Cherokee Nation.

In the next election, Wilma was elected as the first female chief of the Cherokee Nation (and the first female chief of any major Native tribe). She served for 10 years, renewing the tribal government and its relationship with the federal government. She dramatically improved education, housing, and health care while consistently advocating that people in tribal nations have their own indigenous solutions to their problems. For her entire life, she worked for the good of her people.

Her achievements earned her national fame and recognition. She was inducted into the Oklahoma Women's Hall of Fame, was given honorary degrees and a citation for leadership from Harvard University, and was recognized as the Woman of the Year in 1987 by *Ms.* magazine. In 1998, she received the Presidential Medal of Freedom, the nation's highest civilian honor.

In 2010, at the age of 64, Wilma died from pancreatic cancer, but her legacy continues to live on through the doors she opened for other Native American women and the millions of people whom she inspired and cared for.

Blessings to this woman and the wisdom she gave to the world.

You,

Wonderful, Amazing, Gorgeous, Brilliant, Unique, Clever, Sacred, Adorable, Bold, Awesome, Growing, Resilient, Courageous, Determined, Powerful, Miraculous

You.

Meaning: WONDERFUL YOU

Lately, you might have forgotten how wonderful you are. You are a miracle of life itself. You are full of your own wisdom, triumphs, tribulations, and magic. How can you make time to celebrate yourself today? Can you slow down, take a couple of breaths, and acknowledge how far you've come? Give yourself a hug or some other expression of self-love and care.

You matter so much in the balance of the whole world. We are lucky to have you here. Remember, you are a miracle—never let anyone else (or yourself on a low day) convince you otherwise.

Alternate Meaning: SELF-TALK

Your body hears how you talk about yourself. Your heart feels the way you think about yourself. Your soul hears how you imagine yourself. Create a habit of choosing great thoughts about yourself. Become a master of speaking lovingly to yourself.

Your History

Questions to journal or ponder:

Where were you born? What do you love about the place and people you come from?

What were your favorite or defining qualities of yourself as a young child? Are those qualities still alive in you?

What are your greatest accomplishments (so far!)? Against what odds have you triumphed?

What are your favorite qualities of yourself?

What is one loving thing you can tell yourself every day?

What is one thing that excites you about the future of your life?

What mark would you like to leave on the world?